BATTLEGROUND PERTHSHIRE

Best wishes
Rob Hands.

BATTLEGROUND PERTHSHIRE

Two Thousand Years of Battles,
Encounters & Skirmishes

Paul Philippou
&
Rob Hands

TIPPERMUIR
Books

Battleground Perthshire:
Two Thousand Years of Battles, Encounters and Skirmishes.
Copyright © 2009 Paul Philippou and Rob Hands. All rights reserved.

The rights of Paul Philippou and Rob Hands to be identified as the authors
of the Work have been asserted by them in accordance with
the Copyright, Designs and Patents Act 1988.

Published by Tippermuir Books, Perth, Scotland.
www.alternative-perth.co.uk/tippermuirbooks.htm
tippermuirbooks@blueyonder.co.uk

No part of this publication may be reproduced or used in any
form or by any means without written permission from the
Publisher and the authors except for review purposes.

ISBN 978-0-9563374-0-5
A CIP catalogue record for this book is
available from the British Library.

Design and artwork by Bernard Chandler,
Glastonbury, England. www.graffik.co.uk
Illustrations and maps by Rob Hands.
Text set in 9.5pt Janson, with Caslon Open Face titling
and Stempel Garamond running heads.

Printed and bound in Great Britain by
CPI Antony Rowe, Chippenham and Eastbourne

DEDICATION

To Jean, my wife and best friend.

Rob Hands

To Mary, my partner and comrade.

Paul Philippou

As Alexander I will reign,
And I will reign *alone*,
My thoughts did evermore disdain
A rival on my throne.
He either fears his fate too much,
Or his deserts are too small,
That puts it not unto the touch
To win or lose it all.

My Dear and Only Love, I Pray
James Graham, 1st Marquis of Montrose

CONTENTS

ACKNOWLEDGEMENTS

It is our pleasure to acknowledge the help that we have received in the writing of this book. The Local Studies section of the A. K. Bell Library in Perth has been an invaluable archive, without the existence of which we would not have started this project. To Perth and Kinross Council Archives, Perth High School Library, Perth Museum and Art Gallery, Stirling University Library and www.alternative-perth.co.uk we are deeply indebted. To our friend and colleague Jim Hunter, who accompanied us as we walked many of the battlefields, we owe thanks for his insights, knowledge and suggestions.

We wish to express our gratitude to everyone else who has assisted this book from its inception to completion, and particularly Steve Zajda, Jean Hands, Mary Alexander and Peter Dennis for their editorial efforts, and Bernard Chandler whose graphic design skills he has applied so well to improve the visual impact of the book.

Despite all the help and assistance received during the production of this book, we remain entirely responsible for any errors or omissions in the text.

P. P. & R. H.

CHRONOLOGY

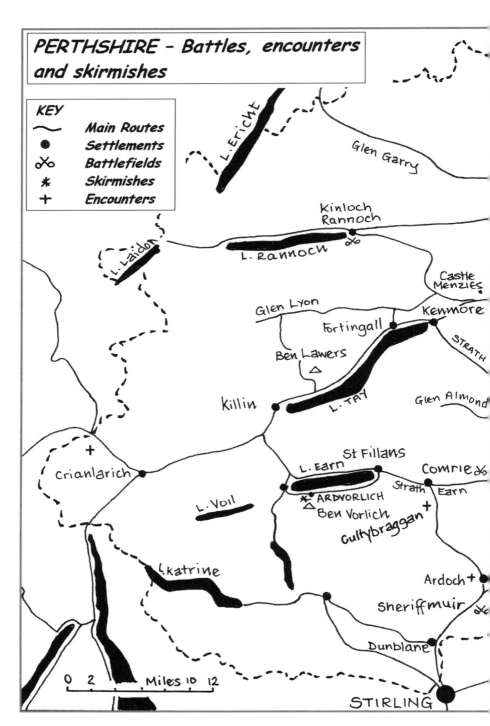

PERTHSHIRE – Battles, encounters and skirmishes

KEY

~	Main Routes
●	Settlements
✂	Battlefields
*	Skirmishes
+	Encounters

L. Ericht

Glen Garry

Kinloch Rannoch ✂

L. Rannoch

L. Laidon

Castle Menzies ●

Glen Lyon

Fortingall

Kenmore ✂

STRATH

Ben Lawers △

Killin ●

L. TAY

Glen Almond

+ Crianlarich ●

St Fillans

L. Earn ●

Comrie ✂

Strath Earn

* ARDVORLICH

△ Ben Vorlich

Cultybraggan +

L. Voil

L. katrine

Ardoch +

Sheriffmuir ✂

Dunblane

0   2   Miles 10   12

STIRLING ●

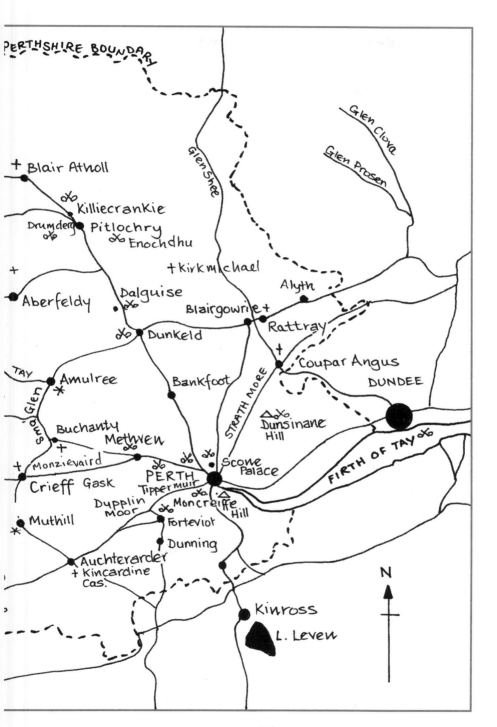

PREFACE

THE 1ST OF SEPTEMBER 1644 was a hot day in Perth for the time of year. It was a Sunday and a cool breeze blowing off the hills made a pleasant addition to a fine day. Several of the town's residents had made their way along the High Street and Longcauseway and after passing the Gin Field, they had settled down by the wide-open plain of Tippermuir. It was their intention to watch their own newly-raised army dispatch an inferior force of Highlanders and Irish mercenaries whose commander they knew to be the Royalist Marquis of Montrose. Looking out across Tippermuir, the Perth folk would have seen a well-equipped army of thousands: musketeers and pikemen deployed in the military fashion of the day, supported by two large cavalry forces, one on each wing. They would have noticed the cannon pointing in the direction of the west and their own Lord Elcho astride his horse directing matters from his army's right wing. Like their troops in front of them, these inquisitive voyeurs would have felt a high degree of confidence as the poorly-armed and rather rag-bag collection of Irish and Highland troops approached. This may have been the last positive thought many of them had. Within minutes of the commencement of fighting, the vast majority of government troops and their officers were in flight. Caught up in this rout were most of the onlookers, who along with a sizeable proportion of the flee-ing army, were hacked down as they ran. This was the Battle of Tippermuir and the first of the many military victories of the Marquis of Montrose.

Tippermuir is the battle that got the two of us started on this project. Discovering that one of the most significant years of the 17th century (in Scotland) began with an event just outside the town in which we lived, made us hungry for more knowledge of both that battle and others of which we were perhaps unaware. After hundreds of hours of research, writing, photography, drawing, discussion, battlefield visits and dozens of pints of very good ale, this desire for the military history of Perth and its environs has led to *Battleground Perthshire*.

1

What we have written is a concise account of most of the battles and minor military events that have taken place within the county of Perthshire. Comprising two thousand years of battles, raids, rebellions, sieges, riots, feuds, ambushes and skirmishes, *Battleground Perthshire* shines the spotlight on the military history of Scotland's big county. Drawn from extensive primary and secondary sources: archives, eyewitness accounts and official records, it tells the fascinating stories of struggles for wealth, power, freedom and the right to self-determination. This chronicle of Perthshire's military history we hope will stand as an important reminder of some of the events that have marked the development of the Scottish people. It will appeal both to the reader interested in the history of Scotland and to those interested in military history.

Whilst every effort has been made to include every battle and military event of the last two millennia within this small book, we have nevertheless been forced by space to make the decision not to include some incidents whose characteristics are more political than military. Within the list of these exclusions are found: significant moments of industrial unrest and strikes at Pullars & Sons Limited (Dyers and Cleaners); the activities of Suffragettes just before the First World War; and the revolutionary actions of strikers during the 1926 General Strike. In addition, we have confined ourselves to battles that have taken place within the historical borders of the county of Perthshire, thus excluding battles that have involved large forces of soldiers raised within the county but fought elsewhere. This means that battles such as that at Flodden in 1513 in which James IV perished alongside two Perthshire earls, a local abbot, dozens of members of the county's aristocracy and hundreds of soldiers enlisted from within Perthshire, although important events within the history of Scotland, do not appear.

Finally, we need to add that the reader may be aware of a military event that has been missed by the authors. We accept full responsibility for any errors and will be delighted to receive information about any omissions so that they can be included in later editions of this book.

CHAPTER I

THE FIRST THOUSAND YEARS

PERTHSHIRE, located as it is north of both Hadrian's Wall and the Antonine Wall, was the northern extremity of Roman Imperial expansion. There are no surviving records of any significant battles that took place within its confines during the opening six centuries of the first millennium AD. In the 18th and 19th centuries, it was, however, a commonly held fallacy that the *Battle of Mons Graupius* (84/85AD) in which Gnaeus Julius Agricola's legions were victorious over the army of the tribes of Caledonia - estimated at 30000 strong - took place either close to the Roman camp at Ardoch, by Braco, or near Comrie, at Dalginross. Current thinking asserts two possibilities: the first that the battle site is near Huntly in Aberdeenshire and the second, that it did not actually take place.

The remains of the Ardoch Roman forts (Alavna Veniconvm - Large/Glen Fort) are north of Braco on the A822. On this site were con- structed several army camps, sizeable earthworks (six feet high in places), forts (5.7-7.2 acres in extent and made of timber and stone), fortlets, an annexe, watch-towers and five or six overlapping marching camps. Agricola's army employed at least one of these marching camps as it travelled north to confront the Caledonians. The fort itself was first constructed c.80AD, rebuilt c.130AD and improved in 158AD. The various camps at Braco were very large;

ROMAN LEGIONARY.

those that were built by Emperor Septimus Severus during his campaigns in Britain (208-211AD) covered 130 acres. Other important Roman military constructions in Perthshire include the forts at Inchtuthill (Pinnata Castra - Large Legionary Fortress by Spittalfield), Dalginross (Medium Fort), Stràgeath (Medium Fort by Innerpeffray), Bertha (Large Fort by the confluence of the River Almond and the River Tay), Carpow (by Newburgh) and the series of watch-towers and encampments along the Gask Ridge.

There is a traditional account of an ***Attack at Lintrose*** (c.84AD) in which a Roman camp, located a few miles south-east of Coupar Angus and comprising three army divisions, was raided by Caledonian tribesmen. The attackers were beaten off and pursued.

The Roman occupiers of the British Isles utilised the term Picts (Painted People) for the loose associations of indigenous tribes that they encountered in the north of the mainland. This amalgam of Iron Age tribes came to dominate and control east and north Scotland between the 4th and the middle of the 9th century. For around three centuries before their ascendancy, the Picts challenged the Roman legions for dominance of the north. The land that became known as Pictland encompassed the territory between Fife and Caithness. By the 6th century, Pictland operated as a unified structure divided into four provinces: Circind (Angus and the Mearns); Fotla (Atholl and Gowrie); Fortriu (Strathearn and Menteith) and Fib (Fife and Kinross). Circind was later divided into a further three kingdoms.

IRON AGE HILL FORT.

Perthshire features significantly in the military history of the Picts, involving battles with forces from both outside and within. The archaeology of this period reveals clues as to the way in which the Picts waged war. Aberlemno churchyard in Aberdeenshire is the location of a Pictish symbol stone upon which can be seen Pictish warriors and their armaments. The warriors illustrated on the stone carry long-shafted spears capable of being employed as either throwing or thrusting weapons and a crossbow-style device. They also carry shields with front-facing bosses. These could be employed defensively or to attack the unguarded heads of opposing warriors. The swords that can be seen on the Aberlemno stone are short broad-bladed types with pommels and

PICTISH WARRIOR.

hilt-guards. Pictish armies included both infantry and cavalry. If the stone engravings are representative of typical formations, Pictish infantry were deployed three ranks deep. The first rank comprised shield men armed with swords who were protected by the spears of the second rank. The third rank was a reserve force armed with spears.

Bordering Pictland to its south and west was the territory of a Gaelic people originating in Ireland, the Scoti. Their kingdom of Dalriada was separated from Pictland by the dorsal ridge mountains, Druim Alban. Scoti territory encompassed County Antrim in Ireland, part of the Inner Hebrides and, by the 6th century, the land of Argyll. Dunadd in the west of Scotland became a major stronghold of the Scoti. As the Scoti expanded eastwards, so they came into conflict with the Picts. Pressure on the Scoti to expand into Pictland came not only from the desire of greater empire but also from external pressure on their territory from the Britons of Strathclyde to the south and Vikings located both north and west of Dalriada. Internal divisions were another motor for conflict within Pictish society and dynastic power struggles were responsible for many battles. Dalriada and Pictland were eventually unified after 843 by Kenneth mac Alpin (Kenneth I).

The earliest recorded battle of this period took place near Dalguise - **Battle of Segues** (635). Of the battle, little is recorded other than it involved an army of the Nechtan dynasty pitched against that of Garnat mac Domnach. Little too is known of the **Battle of Dundurn** (c.683) in which, according to the *Annals of Iona*, an army of Dalriada attacked the Pictish stronghold of Dundurn (pebble or fist fort), located east of St. Fillans upon the rocky hill of Dundurn which rises nearly 300 feet above the adjacent River Earn. A visitor to the site will observe many pebbles, the size of fists, littering the hill. Remnants of a 7th century Pictish oval-shaped nuclear fort survive today; the fort at Dundurn occupied a space 20m by 18m. This hill fort, strategically placed overlooking the routes through Strathearn, was a significant fortress of the Pictish province of Fortriu. Atop the hill was built a centrally-placed citadel surrounded by defensive rings of terraces and walls

DUNDURN HILL FORT.

supported by the hill's natural defensive features. The lower fortifications comprised earthworks. Although the defensive walls are long gone, their remains exist as scree.

In the **Battle of Minvircc** (717) - Glen Falloch (Clach nam Breatann) - an army of invading Britons (from Strathclyde) suffered defeat by the Picts. Around 857, Dunblane became the focus of Briton attention when a raiding army looted the settlement and put it to the torch - **Sack of Dunblane** (c.855-857). Dunblane was sacked again at the start of the 10th century, this time by Danish Vikings. The Danes (led by Rognwald) travelled by ship up the River Tay before marching through Strathearn to undertake the **Second Sack of Dunblane** (912 or 918). On both occasions, Dunblane was destroyed.

At the start of the 8th century, civil war broke out across Pictland. The rivals were provincial kings: Drust, Alpin, Nechtan mac Derile and Oengus mac Forgusso. In 706, Nechtan held the over-kingship; Drust became over-king between 724 and 726 until Alpin succeeded in replacing him. Full-scale war eventually led to the rise of Oengus and the defeat of his rivals.

A force under Oengus attacked and defeated troops under Alpin at the **Battle of Monaidh Croibh** (727-729) - Moncreiffe, by Bridge of Earn - close to the ruined fort that stands on Moncreiffe Hill. This contour fort has a footprint covering almost 4 acres defined by a stone perimeter wall in the centre of which was situated a 40 square metre citadel. Alpin's army was led by one of his sons who was slain during the fighting. Alpin suffered another defeat a year later at a place close to where the River Almond meets the River Tay. In the **Battle of Caislen Credi** (728) victory went to Nechtan and Oengus, who had joined in a temporary alliance. So significant was his defeat,

6

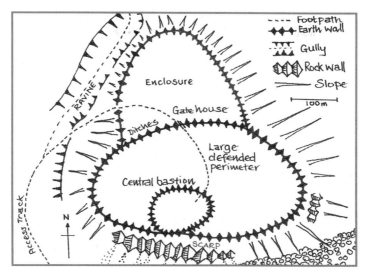

MONCREIFFE HILL FORT.

Alpin fled with the loss of both his territory and his army. The battle site is not far from that of the Pictish royal court of Scone and close to the modern Scone Palace.

The unity between Oengus and Nechtan proved short-lived. Less than a year after their defeat of Alpin, the two kings fought a bloody battle sparked by opposition to Nechtan's tax collecting. There is no conclusive location for

MONCREIFFE HILL.

the **Battle of Monith Carno** (728/729); it most likely took place near Moncur Castle (by Inchture). Oengus' victory ensured that Nechtan's claim to the throne was no longer viable and after the crushing of the last remaining threat, Drust, at the **Battle of Druim Dearg** (12 August 729), the civil war ended with Oengus king of all Pictland, a position he maintained until his death in 761. The *Annals of Ulster* detail the battle as fought half a dozen miles east of Pitlochry at Drumderg (red ridge) by Loch Broom and refer to hillsides littered with dead.

The year 734 witnessed another struggle for the throne when Talorgan mac Drostan attempted to wrestle power from Oengus. Somewhere in the Atholl region, Talorgan's men met an army under Brude mac Oengus - **Battle in Atholl** (734). This challenge was finally resolved in 739 with the execution by ritual drowning of Talorgan. Before his death, Talorgan defeated an army of Dalriada led by Muredach mac Ainfcellach. This **Battle of Cnocc Coirpri** (736) probably took place in the west of Scotland, but the *Annals of Ulster* are ambiguous and it might have been fought in Perthshire. The eastward expansion of Dalriada led to raids on Pictish territory and in 834, a large force of Picts prevented a raid on Dunkeld by meeting the army of Kenneth mac Alpin at Angus. Nine years later, Kenneth mac Alpin succeeded in defeating the Picts under their king, Drust, near Scone - **Battle of Scone** (843). In the **Battle of Strathallan** (878), Aed mac Kenneth was killed in combat and his army defeated by the army of Giric mac Dungal.

Before and after the unification of Pictland and Dalriada, Scotland suffered increasing pressure at the hands of Viking raiders: Norse Vikings from the 8th and Danish Vikings from the 9th century. Viking raids to the Western Isles began in 794; the wealthy religious community of Iona repeatedly plundered from 802 was eventually abandoned in 807. With the building of the church at Dunkeld (c.820), Perthshire, an area of increasing wealth and power, soon became the target of Viking raiders who employed the River Tay to strike deep inland. The first recorded battle against the Vikings in Scotland was the **Battle of Forteviot** (839) in which Pict and Scoti troops, led by Eoganan mac Oengus, his brother Bran and Aed mac Boanta (a sub-king of Dalriada), were defeated by Vikings from Dublin; all three commanders died in the fighting. The battlefield was likely to be close to Forteviot. Kenneth mac Alpin was more successful in 845 when a Viking raiding army intent on plundering Dunkeld was destroyed somewhere between Dunkeld and Clunie Loch. The great sea-faring Viking king, Reguer Lodbog, led this **Attempt on Dunkeld** (845). In 866, a Viking force from Dublin was responsible for the extensive **Raids across Perthshire** (866). It was another sixty years before the Vikings tried their hand at Dunkeld again. In 903 and in 904, Dublin Vikings

VIKING LONGSHIP ON THE TAY, NEAR PERTH.

under their king, Ivarr II, sacked, looted and held Dunkeld, the ecclesiastical centre of Scotland - *Plunder of Dunkeld* (903 and 904).

King Constantine II was defeated by the Danish Vikings at the *Battle of Scone* (904) before finally ending the Viking occupation of Dunkeld at the *Battle of Strathearn* (904-5). This was a complete annihilation of the Vikings, whose king, Ivarr II, was killed in battle.

Very few details are known about the Perthshire battles of the first millennium AD. However, place names act as signs of their existence. The *Battle of Tulloch* (903) is one case in point. In this battle, a Danish Viking raiding army moving westwards across Perthshire was opposed at Tulloch, by Enochdhu (black moor) in Strathardle - a knoll between Kirkmichael and Moulin. The Danes were stopped, and as they fled, they were pursued across the countryside. Near to the battle site, east of Glenfernate Bridge, is a house with the name Tulloch. In the garden of another nearby house (a gatehouse of Dirnanean estate) is a burial mound about 6m long that is associated with the battle. The low mound lies between a 2m standing stone at one end and a small rounded stone at the other. According to legend, the burial mound is that of a local leader, Ardle, who died in the rout of the Danish Vikings after the battle.

Just outside Dunning is a collection of standing stones, one of which is known as Donnchad's Stone and the other as Maormar's Stone. The former of these stones, a rectangular parallelepiped (1.9m high by 0.8m by 1.0m), is reputed to mark the grave of Donnchad, Abbot of Dunkeld, whilst the latter stone (the Gray Stone), a triangular prism (2.1m high by 1.2m by 1.2m by 0.5m), is the reputed burial site of Dub Donn, Earl and Maormar (regional governor) of Atholl, both of whom died during the **Battle of Duncrub** (962- 966). Donnchad's Stone lies in a field north-west of Dunning and Maormar's Stone by Knowes Farm. The name Duncrub is a reference to the ridge (of Crup) which featured in this succession battle between forces loyal to Dubh mac Malcolm (house of Constantine) and those of Culen mac Indulf (house of Aed). Culen's army was the invading force and, in all likelihood, took in an easterly march along Strathearn intent on attacking the royal palace at Forteviot. Before it reached its intended target, Culen's army was met in battle and routed. This was one battle in a series between two families contending for the throne. Only after decades, with the crowning of Malcolm mac Kenneth (Malcolm II), did the feuding end.

The best-known battle against the Vikings, the **Battle of Luncarty** (970, 973, or 990) at Denmarkfield close to Luncarty, did not actually take place. Accounts of this fictional battle describe how men under the flag of Kenneth mac Malcolm (Kenneth II) defeated Danish Vikings fighting for Herveth II, on their way to attack Dunkeld. A stone commonly associated with this battle lies at Luncarty; it is less than a metre in height and carved with images including a crescent-shaped axe.

CHAPTER 2

A NEW MILLENNIUM
&
THE WARS OF INDEPENDENCE

THE START OF THE SECOND MILLENNIUM AD witnessed a new struggle for the throne of Scotland, when Malcolm II, who went on to reign from 1003/5 to 1034, overcame his cousin Kenneth III (Kenneth mac Dubh). In a place between Crieff and Comrie, the armies of the two rivals met in battle - *Battle of Monzievaird* (1003/5). The battle site is likely to have been where Ochtertyre Park is now. An 11th century poem recalls the battle:

The Gael gathered around him,
The day on which he will be killed by us
At his stone of blood between the glens,
Not far from the bends of the Earn.

Above Monzievaird lies a hill, the highest in the area, known as Cairn-Chainachan (cairn of Kenneth) which is traditionally regarded as marking the place where Kenneth III fell.

The most famous of Scottish kings after Robert the Bruce, Macbeth, began his reign in the year 1040 and suffered a serious challenge to his throne on 27 July 1054. An invading army comprising Danish and Northumbrian Anglo-Saxons, and intent on placing Malcolm mac Duncan on the throne of Scotland, marched on and defeated the Scottish king's army at its stronghold by Dunsinnan Hill (Dunsinane Hill) on the western edge of the Sidlaws near Dunkeld. For more than a decade Malcolm, heir to an alternative line to the Scottish throne, had lived in exile in England. His invasion, supported by Edward the Confessor, required his swearing fealty to the English monarch. Nominally, under Malcolm's leadership, the invaders were raised and led by Siward, the Earl of Northumbria, whose personal motivation lay in the hope of annexing the Scottish territory adjacent to his land. The invaders entered Scotland from Northumbria and proceeded to Stirling before marching to

Scone. To supply his army and secure his rear, Siward sent a fleet of ships into the Firth of Tay.

The exact location of the **Battle of Dunsinnan Hill** (27 July 1054) is contested among scholars. Shakespeare's fictional retelling has the battle by Dunsinnan Hill and many historical sources support this theory. Other theories place the battle either between Scone and Dundee or at the confluence of the River Earn and the River Tay. Wherever the actual location may have been, there is general agreement that the battle took place in the open with high casualty levels on both sides. Macbeth's army, though routed from the field, inflicted sufficient casualties on the invaders that they were forced to return home. The *Annals of Ulster* give the casualties as about 3000 for Macbeth's army and around 1500 for the army of Siward. Amongst the losses were Osbeorn, a son of Siward, and Crinan, the Abbot of Dunkeld. The Scot's king, having fled the battle, clung on to power for another three years.

Dunsinnan Hill has been the subject of 'unscientific' archaeological excavation, primarily in the 18th century and the 19th century, with major excavations in 1799 and 1854. In 1857 a dig led by T. M. Nairne, unearthed a bronze double-spiral ring. There are at least two fort constructions at Dunsinnan Hill, the first dating from the Iron Age and the second (inner) fort which was built after the Iron Age.

When Alexander III, king of Scotland, died in an accident near Kinghorn, Fife on 18/19 March 1286, a struggle for control of Scotland began that continued for more than half a century. During that period, the town of Perth witnessed several sieges and several military actions took place within the county borders. Perth spent most of the seventeen years between 1296 and 1313 under English garrison. Improvements made to the town's defences by the garrison included the digging of a new defensive ditch, additions to the walls and the building of several round towers along the perimeter wall.

A consequence of the death of Alexander III was the ascendancy of John Balliol, crowned king on St. Andrew's Day in 1292. Balliol's rise to power, assisted as it was by Edward I of England, required his swearing an oath of allegiance. Despite this oath, two years after his coronation, Balliol refused to send troops to support Edward in his conflict with France. To compound Edward's wrath, Scotland formed an alliance with Philip IV of France. The outcome of this foreign policy was the invasion of Scotland. Berwick-upon-Tweed was sacked and a Scots' army defeated at Dunbar on 27 April 1296. Few Scottish towns dared to resist the victors and just after Stirling Castle came under Edward's control, the town of Perth surrendered without any opposition.

Before long, Balliol was in English hands, imprisoned in the Tower of

London and publicly humiliated. The alliance with France was renounced and landowners throughout Scotland came under obligation to swear allegiance to the English crown. Two Scottish nobles, Andrew Murray and William Wallace, refusing to submit, escaped captivity and returned to Scotland with the aim of maintaining resistance to English rule. A notable early success by Wallace's resistance fighters was the near capture of the English justiciar Sir William Ormesby at Scone in May of 1297. Whilst Ormesby was holding court at Scone, Wallace, together with Sir William Douglas (father of the Black Douglas) and a small group of men, raided Scone. Ormesby, alerted to the attack, escaped only with his life. He was forced to leave behind his possessions and valuables. This *Raid on Scone* (May 1297) was the signal for the commencement of the Scottish uprising.

The year 1297 witnessed other successes for William Wallace in Perthshire. The *Skirmish at Blackford* (1297) was the ambush of a troop of English soldiers attempting to cross the Allan Water near to the village of Blackford. A more substantial victory involved the stronghold of Kinclaven Castle (a garrison castle built between 1220 and 1240 by Alexander II) - *Ambush at Kinclaven* (1297). As a body of English cavalry under the command of Sir James Butler rode out to reinforce the garrison at Kinclaven, Wallace's men set upon them. Butler and many of his men died in the fighting. Those that survived the ambush made their way to Kinclaven Castle, pursued by the Scots. The castle garrison soon surrendered. Kinclaven Castle was burned and its garrison put to the sword. The following day, a force of over a thousand men led by Butler's son, Sir John Butler, marched on Kinclaven. In the *Battle by Kinclaven* (1297), neither side was victorious. Wallace made the tactical decision to go back into hiding and his troops made their way to Methven Wood, travelling firstly through Cargill and Meikleour. In 1336, Scottish troops again captured Kinclaven Castle - *Capture of Kinclaven Castle* (1336) - after which it was dismantled. There is an interpretation plate at the now ruined castle that refers to its wrecking by Wallace and its repair in 1335.

On 11 September 1297, Murray and Wallace, joint leaders of a Scots army, broke the English at Stirling Bridge, though Murray perished after the battle from wounds sustained in the fighting. A soon-knighted Wallace then became the key figure of the Scottish resistance and a Guardian of the Kingdom of King John Balliol. After Edward's return from campaigning in France, a new army was raised in order to re-invade Scotland. The Scots attempted to deny the invaders supplies by destroying the countryside before the English troops could make use of them. Desertions, mutiny and discontent soon became rife in Edward's invasion force. Nevertheless, at Falkirk on 22 July 1298, the Scots, under Sir William Wallace, were defeated. In this battle, Robert the Bruce, later to be Robert I of Scotland, served at Edward's side as his compatriots were driven from the field.

At the end of 1297, Wallace turned his attention to Perth, garrisoned as it was by around 1200 English troops. After a short siege, the town was captured in a bold attack - *Assault on Perth* (end of 1297). A simultaneous attack on two parts of the town's defences allowed a third attack, against a gateway, to succeed. All the English garrison troops were either killed in the fighting or taken prisoner. Sir William Ruthven of Ruthven Castle was appointed Sheriff of Perth and given command of the town. Wallace's troops moved southwards. However, Perth did not remain in Scots hands for very long. Edward I sacked Perth in 1298 as part of his military campaign across Scotland - *Sack of Perth* (1298).

Defeat in the Battle of Falkirk (22 July 1298) forced Wallace to turn to guerrilla warfare, a strategy he continued with until his capture and execution in August of 1305. Just before Wallace was captured, he led his men in a *Skirmish at Earnside* (September 1304), near Bridge of Earn, against a body of English soldiers. This was the last known military action undertaken by William Wallace.

The struggle for the independence of Scotland was also a struggle for the throne. The Guardians of Scotland, Robert the Bruce, John Comyn, the Earl of Carrick and the Earl of Badenoch, each pursued their own interests and allegiances. The intrigue came to a head with the murder by Bruce of John Comyn at Greyfriars Church, Dumfries. With Comyn out of the way, Bruce took the crown of Scotland on 25 March 1306, at Scone.

An ageing Edward I commanded his army to crush the Scots in the most brutal manner possible. Fifteen days after Midsummer a large force assembled at Carlisle before marching on Scotland under the Dragon Banner - the symbol of the absence of mercy. The English army's commander was Aymer de Valance, the 2nd Earl of Pembroke and brother-in-law of the slain John Comyn, appointed by Edward as his Governor of Scotland. Perth was garrisoned in June 1306 by the vanguard of Edward's army.

Robert the Bruce brought his army of veterans, many of whom had served under Wallace, eastwards and reached Perth on 18 June 1306. Inside the town, Aymer de Valance, his officer corps (Henry de Percy, Robert de Clifford, Philip de Mowbray and Sir Ingelram de Umphraville) and the English garrison awaited the Scots' first move. Bruce, wishing to spare Perth, sent forth heralds to negotiate with the garrison commander, the result of which was an agreement to wait until the end of the Sabbath and for the two sides to meet in open battle. Bruce's army then made camp.

The location of Bruce's camp is a matter of conjecture. Methven Den, a wooded spot north of Methven and south of the Almond, is generally now the accepted site for the camp and the **Battle of Methven** (19 June 1306).

THE BATTLE OF METHVEN
19 JUNE 1306

English Army of Edward I
300 Knights (heavy cavalry)
1200-2000 Foot Soldiers

Scots Army of Robert the Bruce
Knights and Foot Soldiers - fewer than the English army

THE BATTLE STORY

THE SCOTS TROOPS, believing the battle with the English garrison to be a day away, relaxed at camp: knights took off their armour, men drank and relaxed without their weapons to hand, and foraging parties went in pursuit of food. Only two-thirds of the Scots army were at the camp when the attack began.

Persuaded by his aide, Umphraville, that open battle against the experienced Scots army was a dangerous and unpredictable gamble, the English commander, de Valance, instead organised a surprise attack. As the light fell, English knights, supported by infantry, fell upon Bruce's men. Warning horns sounded across the Scots' camp, but it was too late. Some of the Scottish knights got to their horses but were unable to organise any defensive formations. Men on the ground were cut down and the battle became a running rout that continued for several days. Although small groups of knights and infantry attempted to make a stand against the superior attacking force, they were no match for troops acting in strength, formation and cohesion.

Bruce himself was captured during the fighting. Luckily, a Scottish knight fighting on the side of the English army (John de Halliburton) recognised the identity of his prisoner. When

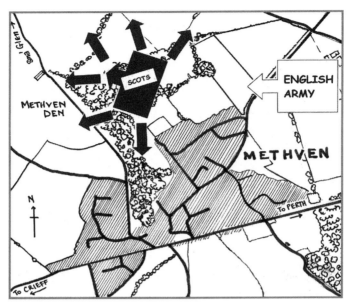

BATTLE OF METHVEN.

a suitable moment arrived Halliburton released the Scottish king who was then able to escape through the woods. Fewer than 500 men escaped the slaughter and pursuit. Many of those captured after the battle were executed. Simon Fraser, a senior figure in the rebellion, was taken to London and publicly executed. The crowd that watched his death was even greater than that which had witnessed the killing of William Wallace. Many other Scottish nobles fell into English hands. Bruce and the remainder of his army crossed the River Tay by Dunkeld (King's Ford) and then the River Garry at Killiecrankie before making their way to Loch Tummel. In June of 2006, the 700th anniversary of the battle was noted by a re-enactment in Methven Park.

Bruce and the Methven survivors rode to the head of Strathfillan then through a mountain pass by Tyndrum. At Dail Righ (King's Field), a low-lying area, they were forced to fight once again - *Fight at Dail Righ* (11-14 August 1306). This time the enemy was loyal to Bruce's old adversaries, the Comyns: Sir John MacDougall, Lord of Lorn (chief of Clan MacDougall and uncle to John Comyn whom Bruce had murdered earlier that year), several barons of Argyll and 1000 armed men (MacDougalls and Macnabs). During the mêlée, Bruce was almost killed when a MacDougall soldier grabbed his plaid. Only by ridding himself of his vestment did Bruce prevent himself being dragged towards the swords of his enemy.

The battle at Dail Righ was a disaster for Bruce. Once again he was defeated and now no longer commanded a viable military force. With very few horse and men at his disposal, Robert the Bruce made the tactical decision to split his party, sending the queen and his daughter on the remaining horses to attempt to reach Kildrummy Castle on Donside. He placed them under the protection of his brother Neil, Earl of Atholl, whilst he and his few remaining men hid in the Perthshire hills.

Bruce's small band hid at first in Glen Falloch and later in a cave by Inversnaid. Whilst Bruce and his men moved from hiding place to hiding place, the Lord of Lorn scoured the countryside seeking a bloody revenge for John Comyn's death. After discovering Bruce's whereabouts as being in the Kinloch Rannoch area, the Lord of Lorn moved into Rannoch from the south with a large body of troops including a contingent of English regulars. Donnachadh Reamhar (Duncan the Stout), the local clan chief, raised

ROBERT THE BRUCE.

the Fiery Cross (crois taraidh) at Fea Choire (the assembly place - a glen running between Rannoch and Glenerochty) and gathered his clan to protect their king. At the point where the glen opened out into the lowlands at Loch Rannoch's eastern extent, the two armies met in combat - **Battle of Innerhadden** (late summer 1306). This running battle began at Innerhadden and continued to Dalchosnie (Field of Victory) where Bruce and his allies were victorious. The English troops fled the field via Glen Sassunn and to this day this glen is known as the Glen of the English.

Sir John MacDougall returned one more time to Rannoch in pursuit of Bruce. Approaching from the north-west, Lorn camped his men a couple of miles from Loch Rannoch. According to legend, Duncan the Stout entered Lorn's camp in disguise but, being discovered, was forced to run for his life. Only a superhuman leap of 16 feet across a river (Leum Donnachadh - Stout Duncan's Leap) enabled the Duncan clan chief to avoid capture. The following morning, Duncan led his men in a surprise attack on the MacDougall camp - *Skirmish by Loch Rannoch* (late summer 1306). Very soon overcome, the MacDougalls scattered in an attempt to escape. Many were captured, amongst them their military commander, Alexander MacDougall. Duncan had his high-profile captive locked away in an island stronghold at the western extremity of Loch Rannoch - the Isle of the Gulls. It was not until 1314 when they joined his army in defeating the English at Bannockburn that Stout Duncan and his clan warriors met Bruce again.

After Methven Bruce followed Wallace's tactics, employing guerrilla warfare and both small and large scale military operations to wear down the English occupation troops. These actions were not confined to Scotland: England itself was raided as far south as Yorkshire.

In February 1311, Piers Gaveston, 1st Earl of Cornwall, was sent by Edward II with a strong force of Scottish soldiers loyal to the English crown to occupy Perth and disrupt Bruce's ability to operate north of the Forth. The town's defences were improved once more. In October 1311, Sir William Oliphant, an experienced military commander, after having spent four years imprisoned in England, accepted Edward's offer to command the garrison at Perth. Sir William Oliphant had previously been in the service of King John Balliol.

From its low point, the Scottish struggle might well have ended. Yet, eight years later at Bannockburn (24 June 1314), an English army was defeated and the wars of independence entered their final stage. Scotland achieved its independence in 1328 when Edward III was forced to surrender his northern kingdom and renounce his claim to Scotland.

The *Recapture of Perth* (8 January 1313) was led by Robert the Bruce himself. He is said to have personally led his troops across Perth's water-filled moat and was the second man to gain entry to the town. The attack on the English garrison began at the end of the previous year. For six weeks, the Scots laid siege but failed in their attempts to breach the surrounding wall. The besiegers then withdrew from the vicinity of Perth and hid nearby. A week after the siege was lifted, the garrison relaxed its guard. A surprise attack was launched on the night of the 7-8 of January. The attacking troops, only lightly armed and armoured, were able to cross the fosse and scale the walls. Very soon the town was taken. Several Scottish nobles and burghers of Perth who had worked with the occupiers were executed under Bruce's order. Perth remained in Scottish hands for twenty years. State (Exchequer) records show that King Robert was a frequent visitor to Perth after its liberation and rented accommodation for both himself and his pet lion.

As with the death of Alexander III, the loss of the king of Scotland in 1329 was the opportunity for those with designs on the Scottish crown to re-emerge and try to take centre-stage. The new king of Scotland, David II, was only four years old. This time the contender for the throne was Edward Balliol, son of King John Balliol. Funded by Edward III and with the assistance of most of the exiled Scottish barons and nobles (those who had lost their Scottish lands in the wars of independence) Balliol organised an invasion army of English troops and foreign mercenaries. The operational commander of the army was Henry Lord Beaumont, an experienced soldier who had fought at Falkirk and Bannockburn.

A fleet of ships left the English ports of Ravenser, Barton and Hull on 31 July 1332, and deposited the invaders at Kinghorn, Fife, on 6 August 1332. Opposition to the landing was minor and a local militia force commanded by Duncan, Earl of Fife, was easily overcome. Balliol's army needed a day to unload supplies before moving inland, firstly to capture Dunfermline and then Scone, travelling by way of Loch Leven, the Ochils, the Water of May and Forteviot before reaching the River Earn three days later. At the Earn, the passage of the invaders was halted by the presence of a huge Scottish army camped near Dupplin Castle (a strong tower), on the Gask Ridge, commanded by the King's Regent, the Earl of Mar. Balliol occupied one side of the Earn (Miller's Acre by Forteviot) and Mar the other. The bridge was controlled by Scottish troops. A second Scottish army, that of the Earl of March, lay at Auchterarder. Balliol had no choice but to fight the nearer of the two armies before they could unite.

In the meantime, the English fleet sailed up the Tay Estuary to offer an escape route if required and to supply the invaders should they manage to reach Perth.

The night before the **Battle of Dupplin Moor** (11-12 August 1332), Beaumont ordered Alexander Mowbray and a small party of men to attack a section of the Scottish camp. The attack was successful and caused some disruption in the Scots army. The main part of Balliol's army located a ford at Dalreoch and crossed the Earn before deploying for the battle to come.

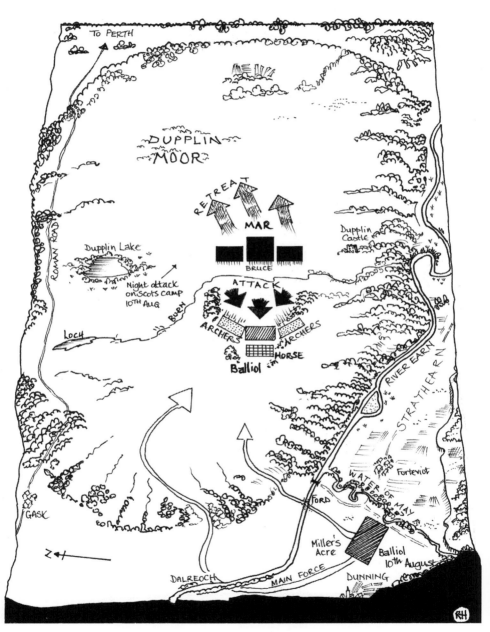

BATTLE OF DUPPLIN MOOR.

THE BATTLE OF DUPPLIN MOOR
11-12 AUGUST 1332

Edward Balliol's Army
3300-3500 Men (some sources suggest as low as 1500-2000)
40 Horsemen (Dutch/Flemish mercenaries)

Earl of Mar's Army
5000-6000 Infantry (some sources suggest up to 30000 troops)
1200 Men-at-Arms
800 Horse
58 Knights
18 Knight Bannerettes

POSSIBLE LOCATION OF THE BATTLE OF DUPPLIN MOOR.

THE BATTLE STORY

LORD BEAUMONT arranged his force between the narrow passage of a glen with steep wooded banks, thus protecting his wings and forcing the numerically superior enemy to fight on a reduced frontage. Beaumont next deployed his troops in three tiers: the front layer of three ranks of dismounted men-at-arms; the second, four ranks of infantry; the rear tier of spearmen. Behind them, he positioned his archers and finally guarded his rear with his mounted mercenaries. The front ranks were protected from

BATTLE OF DUPPLIN MOOR.

cavalry by the protruding spears of his spearmen; Bannockburn had taught Beaumont about the susceptibility of troops to cavalry charge. In front of Balliol's army, on Dupplin Moor, the Scots army prepared to attack.

An overconfident Scottish army formed up in either two or three huge and unwieldy schiltrons. Robert the Bruce's Battalion (led by his illegitimate son, Robert Bruce) took the front. Disagreement amongst the Scottish commanders caused tactical confusion that only added to the failures of that day.

The Scots advanced on Balliol's defensive line and, as they approached, the English longbow men began the dominance that their weaponry would wield in war for the next century. Arrows rained down on the unprotected heads and faces of the advancing Scottish troops inflicting terrible injuries. Still Mar's army continued with the attack. Very soon, the first Scottish schiltron made contact with the frontline. Sheer weight of numbers and pressure forced Balliol's men back thirty feet, but they did not yield. All the while, the Scots pressed forward, arrows were causing havoc across their lines. Mar sent all his troops into action, even his reserve battalions, believing that the English line would break. These further troops and the effectiveness of the English longbow men broke up Mar's formations and added a crushing pressure on those at the front. Men fighting in the very front were pressed on English spears, crushed underfoot by their own men or, falling, became easy targets for the English spearmen.

Eventually, Mar's army broke and fled the field. Beaumont then deployed his small cavalry unit who harried the fleeing Scots. Both the Earl of Mar and Robert Bruce fell in the battle and the command of the Scots army fell to the Earl of Fife. His attempt to organise an orderly retreat failed and he was captured. As well as the army command, the Scots losses were in the thousands (sources give figures from 2000 to 13000) and included the Earl of Moray, the Earl of Menteith, Alexander Fraser and Sir Robert Keith, the hero of Bannockburn.

For many years, a 9th century Pictish standing stone, known as the Dupplin Cross, was considered as a marker of the Battle of Dupplin Moor. It is now housed in St. Serf's Church in Dunning. There is no evidence with which to locate the actual battle site. It may have been near to the Dupplin Cross; equally, it may have been to the west at Upper Cairnie. There are a number of deep ditches on Dupplin Moor traditionally associated with the battle casualties.

A victorious Balliol marched his army to Perth where the town opened its doors to him on 13 August 1332. Aware that the second Scots army of 30000 men under the Earl of March, the Earl of Dunbar and Sir Archibald Douglas was approaching Perth, Balliol ordered a strengthening of fortifications (reduced by Robert the Bruce in 1313) and the building of palisades.

BATTLE OF THE TAY ESTUARY.

March's soldiers marched across Dupplin Moor before deploying on high ground outside the town. Perth was surrounded. The Scots prepared for an assault by cutting large quantities of brush and branch at Lammerkin Wood to fill the defensive moat and yet the order to attack was never given. The Scots dug in and the battle for Perth moved to the Tay Estuary.

Although Perth was surrounded, the English fleet deployed at the mouth of the River Tay supplied the town. The Scots called upon the services of a renowned mercenary sea captain, John Crabbe. Crabbe brought his fleet of ten Flemish ships from Berwick-upon-Tweed, reaching the River Tay on 24 August 1332. The ***Battle of the Tay Estuary*** (24 August 1332) began immediately. Initially Crabbe was successful: the main ship in the English fleet, Beaumont's cog, a vessel of 200-250 tons, was captured easily. It seemed the superior mercenary ships would take the day. Yet the English seamen fought like devils and not only saw off the attack but inflicted significant losses on Crabbe's squadron. Many of the Flemish vessels were set alight and John Crabbe himself was forced to walk back to Berwick-upon-Tweed.

This setback, compounded with March's difficulty in providing for so many men in the field, persuaded the Scots commander to withdraw from Perth. Far to the south, in Galloway, troops loyal to Balliol, commanded by Eustace Maxwell of Caerlaveroch, were on the march and so the Scots army moved to meet them. By September of 1332 Balliol, having made the decision to support the Galloway rising, garrisoned Perth and marched south. Before he left he was crowned at Scone (24 September 1332). He remained king for only a few weeks. His camp at Annan was subject to a surprise attack by a force under Sir Archibald Douglas. Balliol and his remaining supporters fled to England where they would begin to plot their next adventure north of the border.

Perth's new commander was the Earl of Fife who had joined Balliol after the defeat at Dupplin Moor. Very little time elapsed before Sir Simon Fraser, John Lindsay and Sir Robert Keith (son of the Robert Keith killed at Dupplin Moor) re-secured the town in the name of David II. There was very little real fighting involved with this attack and the Earl of Fife was given only a token prison sentence for his temporary shift in loyalty. Once more Perth's defences were reduced.

Within a year, Balliol was back in Scotland alongside Edward III, his Lord Paramount, and with a new invasion force. The Scots dispatched Sir Archibald Douglas with an army to relieve the English siege of Berwick-upon-Tweed. Just outside Berwick-upon-Tweed, the two armies met and the Scots were crushed - ***Battle of Halidon Hill*** (19 July 1333). As part of the English re-occupation of Scotland, Perth was again garrisoned. Utilising money forcibly extracted from the town's religious houses, Perth's fortifications were improved. They were tested in the summer of 1339.

Resistance to English rule continued throughout the occupation, so by the time of the 1339 *Siege of Perth* (1399), much of Scotland had been liberated. However, the English garrison commander, Sir Thomas Ughtred, had no reason to feel insecure about his position. A lade protected the town on three sides. The River Tay secured its fourth and enabled supplies to be brought by ship. A new *Battle of the Tay Estuary* (1339) followed. Hugh Hardpile, a French pirate, and his fleet of five mercenary ships, was commissioned to disrupt the English supply vessels in and around the Firth of Tay.

The Scots commanders, the Earl of Ross and Sir William Douglas of Lothian, now applied themselves to the assault of Perth. Brushwood was thrown into the Lade as its level fell dramatically after its feed, the River Almond, was diverted. The date for the assault of Perth was set for 7 July, but the operation coincided with an eclipse of the sun and so the attack was abandoned. This allowed Sir Thomas Ughtred to reassess his precarious situation and so enter into surrender talks with the besieging forces. Ughtred and his garrison were allowed to leave Perth safely and return to England on their ships, which had been anchored downstream.

By 1341 the whole of Scotland was liberated and King David returned from exile in France. The wars of independence were at an end.

CHAPTER 3

THE ENGLISH CIVIL WAR
& THE WARS OF
THE THREE KINGDOMS

THE ENGLISH CIVIL WAR began in 1642 and was, in the main, a struggle for domination of the political, economic and religious life of that country. Scotland, although lagging behind England economically and politically, had thrown off the shackles of the established church and aristocracy by 1642. The attempt by Charles I to control the Church of Scotland and re-appropriate church land met with revolt in his northern kingdom. In February of 1638, the writing of the National Covenant set the stage for a major conflict between the Scottish and English realms. This proceeded in earnest in January 1644 when the Army of the Solemn League and Covenant invaded England with 18000 infantry, 3000 horse and 500-600 dragoons. A second invasion was undertaken in June 1644, this time with only 6800-8000 troops. After the defeat of the Royalists and the execution of Charles I (30 January 1649), the first stage of the civil war ended.

The period 1644 to 1746 saw Perthshire at the heart of a nation in turmoil over its political future. The period begins in the aftermath of the Bishops' War (1639-40). It is deeply affected by the English Civil War, the Wars of the Three Kingdoms and a series of risings for the Stuart cause and ends with the defeat of that cause at Culloden in 1746. Events, often on Perthshire soil, were at the hub of the upheavals that haunted Scotland at the time and were significant in terms of the developing United Kingdom and the modern British state.

The *Battle of Tippermuir* (1 September 1644) is a highly significant battle in a key period of Scottish history as it represents the beginning of the campaign waged by James Graham, 1st Marquis of Montrose, in support of Charles I against the Covenanter controllers of Scotland led by Archibald Campbell, the 1st Marquis of Argyll. Close links to Perthshire permeate this campaign because the Marquis of Montrose had his established power base in the Graham lands between Auchterarder and Montrose in Angus.

Following the defeat suffered by Charles I by the English Parliamentary Army at Marston Moor (2 July 1644) in which the Scots Covenanter Army played a decisive role, Montrose sought to ease pressure on the King's forces in England by rallying Royalist support in Scotland, primarily to draw Scottish troops back from England and Ireland. Randal McDonnell, the Marquis of Antrim, promising 10000 Irish troops for a campaign against the Covenanters in Scotland, provided between 2000 and 2500. Landing, initially, on the Ardnamurchan peninsula (west coast of Scotland) on 8 July 1644 under the leadership of Alasdair MacColla, the intention of joining up with the Royalist forces of the Marquis of Huntly was thwarted by the failure of the Gordon's rising in the North-East. Failure to raise sympathetic but cowed Northern clans to the cause and pressure from advancing Campbell forces under Argyll forced the beleaguered Irish troops south into Atholl.

Meanwhile, Montrose with two followers had moved north across the border with the King's Warrant as Lieutenant Governor of Scotland. Having arrived in Perthshire in late August and whilst in hiding in Methven Wood, word arrived of MacColla's Irish and Highland army now encamped at Blair Castle, which had been abandoned by Covenanter forces on 9 August. Montrose and Patrick Graham of Inchbrackie (known as Black Pate) hurried to Blair to take command of the Royalist army, arriving in the nick of time to prevent a battle between MacColla's army and the gathered Robertsons and Atholl men determined to repulse the invaders - *Stand-off at Blair Castle* (29 August 1644).

Montrose was known locally and was recognised. Displaying the Royal Warrant giving him the King's authority, he drew together and formed the nucleus of an army that was to sustain him in a military campaign lasting just over a year between 1644 and 1645. That night and the next day a council of war decided to move on Perth rather than Stirling where Argyll's forces were gathering. With the Royal Standard (a Scarlet Lion) raised behind Blair Castle, Montrose and MacColla moved their army by the way of the River Garry and River Tay through the Menzies lands between Pitlochry and Aberfeldy in the hope of gaining more support from Castle Menzies. Instead, the local clansmen harried the moving columns and the Menzies refused to support the Royalist cause. The Irish troops in return harried the local population and burned standing crops en route to Aberfeldy - *Burning of Weem* (30/31 August). An *Attack on Castle Menzies* (30/31 August) ended in failure.

From Aberfeldy, the logical approach to Perth was by way of the Sma' Glen and it was here at Buchanty Hill by the River Almond on 31 August that a force of 600 men, local levies, under John Graham (Lord Kilpont) and Sir John Drummond, were charged with guarding the route to Perth. Kilpont, a kin of Montrose, outnumbered by the approaching force, resolved to join the Royalist cause - *Stand-off at Buchanty Hill* (31 August 1644). It is not clear whether Kilpont and Montrose planned this move all along. The defection of Stewart of Ardvorlich soon after the Battle of Tippermuir suggests that not all of Kilpont's men were convinced in declaring for the King. Continuing south-west towards Crieff, Montrose camped overnight on the Moor of Fowlis on the eve of the battle.

Argyll, with a considerable force gathered at Stirling, threatened the Royalist forces from the west. For Montrose and MacColla, it was imperative to prevent Argyll's army joining with the force assembling in Perth under David Wemyss, Lord Elcho. Lacking in supplies and ammunition for the Irish and Highland troops, Montrose decided to take Perth and therefore meet Elcho's superior army, with the supplies in Perth an obvious prize in the enfolding campaign. Montrose's approach to Perth from Fowlis Moor would likely have used the old Perth-Crieff road, known at its Perth end as the Old Gallows Road. Montrose stopped at Tibbermore Church. Perth Presbytery accounts in the aftermath of the battle record that the Minister of Tibbermore Church, Mr Balnevis, was censured for giving the Marquis of Montrose a glass of water before the battle. On the other side, Lord Elcho brought his Covenanter forces out of Perth by the Burghmuir to occupy the Ridge of Lamberkine and protect the approach to the town.

PIKEMEN AT TIPPERMUIR.

Battle tactics of the time were relatively consistent. Civil War armies utilised match-lock or flintlock guns and pikes in massed formations normally six deep. This number was dictated by the military operation known as the counter-march where a rank of six musketeers lined up one behind the other. The front man fired and moved to the rear of the column and reloaded as he moved again towards the front in turn. In this war, well-drilled troops could mount continuous and effective fire as the two armies closed on each other to the point at which both sets of pike men engaged each other in the so-called push of pike. Close quarter hand-to-hand fighting ensued until one army's line was breached or pushed back and the army broke.

Alasdair MacColla's Irish troops employed a different tactic, one that had been a success in the fighting in Ireland. This involved what became known as the Highland Charge. This method would be used again several times and usually successfully in the next hundred years. However, it was probably at Tibbermore the tactic was first recorded as utilised in mainland Scotland.

THE BATTLE OF TIPPERMUIR
1 SEPTEMBER 1644

Royalist Army of Charles I
c.3100 infantry
Colonel Patrick Graham of Inchbrackie's Perthshire Levies:
(Athollmen - Stewarts, Robertsons, Camerons and Murrays) 500
Major Thomas Laghtnan's Regiment: (Irish) 700
Colonel James McDonnell's Regiment: (Irish) 400
Colonel Manus O'Cahan's Regiment: (Irish) 400
Ewan Og MacPherson's Badenoch Battalion: (levies) 500
Lord Kilpont's Perthshire Levies:
(Lowlanders - West Perthshire and Menteith) 500
MacDonald of Keppoch's unit: (irregulars) 100

Covenanter (Government) Army
1900-2300 infantry
400-600 cavalry
Earl of Tullibardine's Regiment: (Angus & Fife - regulars) 600-800
Lord Elcho's Regiment: (regulars) 500
Dundee and Forfarshire Levies: 600-800
Perth Trained Band: (militia) 200
Sir James Scott of Rossie's Regiment:
(Clackmannanshire & Fife - cavalry) 200-300
Lord Elcho's Regiment:
(Clackmannanshire & Fife - cavalry) 200-300
2-9 pieces of artillery (3-pounders or 5-pounders)

THE BATTLE STORY

THE TWO ARMIES were roughly the same size, but Elcho's command had a distinct advantage of 300 cavalry on each wing. This gave the Covenanters protecting Perth a longer line and threatened the Royalist flanks. Montrose therefore extended his line by lining up his flank regiments, Kilpont on the right and the Athollmen under his own command on the left, three deep instead of the normal six deep. MacColla's three regiments formed the centre of the Royalist formation.

The Covenanter centre was commanded by James Murray, 2nd Earl of Tullibardine, and made up of the Tayside levies, while Lord Elcho, as overall commander, controlled the right wing cavalry facing Lord Kilpont. Sir James Scott of Rossie, an experienced professional officer, led the left wing cavalry formation. Elcho had as many as nine artillery pieces facing the enemy.

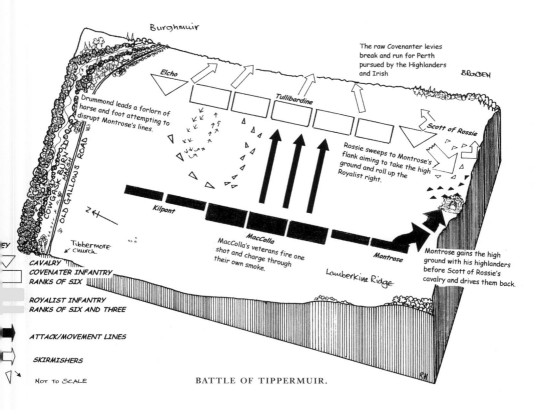

The raw Covenanter levies break and run for Perth pursued by the Highlanders and Irish

Drummond leads a forlorn of horse and foot attempting to disrupt Montrose's lines.

Rossie sweeps to Montrose's flank aiming to take the high ground and roll up the Royalist right.

MacColla's veterans fire one shot and charge through their own smoke.

Montrose gains the high ground with his highlanders before Scott of Rossie's cavalry and drives them back.

CAVALRY
COVENATER INFANTRY RANKS OF SIX
ROYALIST INFANTRY RANKS OF SIX AND THREE
ATTACK/MOVEMENT LINES
SKIRMISHERS
NOT TO SCALE

BATTLE OF TIPPERMUIR.

The formalities of battle involved an approach by David Drummond, the Master of Madderty, to Elcho's lines under a flag of truce. Montrose revealed his Royal Authority as Lieutenant Governor of Scotland to try to persuade the Covenanters to submit to the King. He also suggested a delay so as not to fight on the Sabbath. The ministers attached in some numbers to Elcho's army replied, *"What better day to do the Lord's work?"* The Covenanter army was driven by religious zeal and served under the slogan, *'Jesus and no quarter'*. The seizing of Montrose's envoy and his manhandling off to Perth to await execution after the battle inflamed the situation.

The battle began with Tullibardine sending out a *forlorn hope* of musketeers and horse from his centre led by Colonel James Drummond. This was a standard tactic at the time and involved a small group moving towards their enemy (within a hundred feet or more) and across its front firing pistols as they went in the hope of disrupting their formation and creating an opportunity to exploit. The experienced Irish held their line and the *forlorn hope* was driven back towards their own lines creating confusion in the centre as they did so. This prompted decisive action from Montrose whose troops, short of ammunition, were ordered forward, fired a single volley at about 20 to 30 paces and charged through their own smoke with sword, targe and dirk in hand or with clubbed muskets. This

TIBBERMORE CHURCH.

so unnerved the raw, inexperienced government soldiers that they immediately broke and the battle became a rout. Neither Elcho nor Kilpont on their side of the battlefield seem to have engaged. Montrose made a dash for the high ground on his right just gaining its advantage ahead of Scott of Rossie's cavalry. Firing a single volley at them, they failed to drive them back but attacked the horsemen and their mounts by charging down the slope at them, even throwing stones to add to the ferocity of their attack. A fierce fight developed but Rossie's men proved no match for Montrose's Highlanders and were driven back.

Elcho's whole line had now crumbled and was fleeing for the safety of Perth in confusion with riders driving through disorganised infantry who were abandoning their weapons. Some of the townsfolk of Perth who had come out to watch the battle were caught up in the retreat. The numbers of Covenanter casualties vary according to source but as many as 1000 dead were left on the battlefield and on the line of retreat that ran towards Broxden and Needless Road seeking either the safety of Pitheavlis Castle or the walls of Perth. Accounts suggest that up to 300 Covenanters lie in an unmarked grave in Tibbermore Churchyard. Estimates of prisoner numbers vary wildly. Most likely they were around the 300 to 400 mark. During the Royalist occupation of Perth, the Covenanter prisoners were held in St. John's Kirk. The Royalist casualty level was very low at a few dozen killed.

After the battle, the bodies of around 90 Fife levies were discovered in a field close to and north of the hamlet of Needless (near Needless Road/ Wilson Street) and so buried nearby. A stone was erected to mark the burial spot. It has since disappeared. Upon the wall of a house at the corner of Needless Road and Wilson Street is fixed a modern plaque that bears testament to the Battle of Tippermuir and the burial of the soldiers from Fife.

Perth Museum and Art Gallery is in possession of one of two banners known to have belonged to the Glovers Incorporation of Perth. This banner (dated 1604) may have accompanied the thirteen glovers who served as musketeers within the Perth Militia section of the Covenanter army that was defeated at Tippermuir. According to the *Annals of the Glovers Incorporation of Perth*, the glovers (Thomas Dundee, Alexander Kinnaird, Alexander Nairne, George Auchenlick, William Gell, James Masone, Henry Paul, Alexander Hutton, Patrick Inglis, Andrew Mortimer, Robert Lamb, Andrew Anderson [ensign] and Alexander Drummond [lieutenant]) marched out to meet the Royalists under their captain, David Grant, displaying their Ancient Corporation's banner. Captain Grant was killed in the battle.

With the defeat of the Government army, Perth lay open to the Royalist troops. The magistrates of Perth tried in vain to raise a force to defend the town, so instead gave the keys of Perth to Montrose and MacColla - *Capture of Perth* (9 September 1644). A deal was struck between the town's leaders and Montrose, which saw to the protection of the town and its citizens. The Royalist army remained at Perth for four days during which period it appropriated equipment and money. Several prominent members of the Covenanter army chose to go over to the Royalist cause, amongst them Lord Drummond and Oliphant of Gask. There was also one significant defection from the Royalists: Stewart of Ardvorlich stabbed and killed his friend, Lord Kilpont, before fleeing to the Covenanter side for protection.

During his army's presence in Perthshire, Montrose lay siege to and captured a castle belonging to the Campbells - *Siege of Sybilla Island Castle* (1644). The castle was located on Sybilla Island (Priory Island or Eilean Nam Ban) on Loch Tay's southern side.

Tippermuir was the beginning of Montrose's year of miracles during which his army marched the length and breadth of Scotland inflicting defeat after defeat on Covenanter armies - Battle of Aberdeen (Justice Mills), 13 September 1644; Battle of Inverlochy, 2 February 1645; Battle of Auldearn, 9 May 1645; Battle of Alford, 2 July 1645 and Battle of Kilsyth, 15 August 1645 - before being beaten at the *Battle of Philiphaugh* (13 September 1645). A year later, Charles I as a prisoner of Parliament, commanded Montrose to cease hostilities. Montrose, then based at Blairgowrie, disbanded his army and went into exile.

Charles II formed an alliance with the Scottish Presbyterians in 1650 and was subsequently crowned King of Scots at Scone on 1 January 1651, having agreed to subscribe to the Solemn League and Covenant. Despite an appeal by Cromwell to the Assembly of the Church of Scotland, the alliance with the Crown remained. A force of veteran soldiers was then dispatched to invade Scotland. The invasion went poorly at first and by 3 September 1650 Cromwell was poised to evacuate his army by sea from Dunbar. Running short of supplies, the Parliamentarian troops had failed to make significant inroads against the Scottish army led by General Leslie. The Battle of Dunbar was a major change in the invaders' fortune. Four thousand Scottish soldiers were killed at Dunbar and 10000 were captured. The defeat of Leslie left the road to Edinburgh open and the Scottish capital was soon captured. As Cromwell made progress in Scotland, the Burgh of Perth made the decision to send 100 men under the command of Captain Andrew Butter, Lieutenant John Davidson and Ensign James Dyke to join a Scots army mobilising at Dunfermline. As a column of Parliamentarian troops command-ed by Major General John Lambert pushed into Fife, General Leslie ordered Sir John Browne of Fordell and Major General Holbourne to take their army of 4000 Covenanters from Dunfermline to oppose the invaders. The govern-ment army was obliterated, losing over 1600 men. Perth was left exposed. The surviving Perth troops returned home to warn of an impending attack. Meanwhile, Charles II left Stirling with his army and the intention of leading an attack on England.

On 3 August 1651, General Monck arrived at the gates of Perth at the head of his troops. Inside the town, Lieutenant Davidson ordered the militia to bang drums and make the sounds of military manoeuvres so that the approaching army be put off attempting to assault the town. This was successful and surrender terms were offered, which were accepted. The *Capture of Perth* (3 August 1651) was completed without any bloodshed. As Cromwell and his men entered Perth, the Provost, Andrew Grant, greeted them. Cromwell quizzed the Provost and Lieutenant Davidson as to how they intended to defend the town with so few troops. Their answer was that the Burghers intention was only to hold up the English army to allow the King to escape south. This earned the Provost a serious dressing down and nearly led to the hanging of Lieutenant Davidson. Cromwell's interaction with Davidson occurred in the latter's home which, bizarrely, partially collapsed just after Cromwell had left.

Perth's South Inch was selected as one of five national locations (Ayr, Inverlochy, Inverness, Leith and Perth) at which fortified citadels were to be constructed as a means of controlling Scotland. In order to build Perth's citadel, the town was vandalised: stones and materials were stripped from most secular and non-secular buildings - the hospital, bridge, several houses, the Mercat Cross and Greyfriars burial ground. The town itself underwent major fortification; it was garrisoned for the next seven years. The citadel (built in 1652) was a sizeable construction: off-square with sides around 266 feet long, with a bastion standing at each

CROMWELL'S TROOPS AT
ST. JOHN'S KIRK.

vertex. A moat circumscribed the citadel so that a pier was required to bring supplies from ships on the River Tay into the citadel. Cromwell's citadel

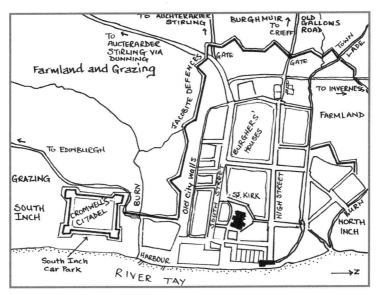

PERTH c.1716, SHOWING LOCATION OF CROMWELL'S CITADEL
AND THE JACOBITE DEFENCES.

remained standing until 1661, at which time Charles II granted a charter to
Perth to demolish the citadel and distribute its materials to the citizens of the
town. The ditch around the citadel remained visible until the 18th century,
but today there are no observable remains. An interpretation board giving
details of the citadel is located in the middle of the South Inch car park.

During the occupation and subjugation of Scotland, a few incidents of note
involving Cromwell's army occurred in Perthshire. The first, the ***Raid on Scone***
(28 August 1651) in which 800 cavalry troopers raided Scone and almost
captured the Committee of Estates (Scottish government) had it been successful, might have had a dramatic historical effect. A month later, the boot
was on the other foot when 300 Scots troops ambushed and captured a small
troop of Cromwellian soldiers just outside Perth - ***Ambush near Perth***
(12 September 1651). The next incident of note involved troops billeted at
Kirkmichael. An officer of the occupying army unit was killed by the brother
of a girl that he had been harassing. Once word reached that officer's men,
they began to search the village with the intention of seeking revenge. As the
soldiers hunted for the killer, the other local men were at prayer in the Old
Kirk. The alarm was raised in the church and the men of Kirkmichael rose as
one and came out to fight. It is not clear as to who the victors were in the
Fight at Kirkmichael (1653) - many were injured on both sides. Whilst the

fighting raged in the village, the dead officer's body was taken away by the locals and buried in a hollow. This later became known locally as Lag an't Sassenach (Hollow of the Englishman). In 1654, General Monck besieged and captured the small castle on Sybilla Island, the largest island in Loch Tay - *Siege of Sybilla Island Castle* (1654).

In addition, both Blair Castle and Drummond Castle were attacked by Cromwell's army - *Attack on Blair Castle and Drummond Castle* (1653).

CHAPTER 4

THE HOUSE OF STUART
&
THE JACOBITE REBELLIONS

IN 1688, in what became known as the Glorious Revolution, the English monarch James II (VII of Scotland) was deposed by Parliament in favour of his son-in-law, William of Orange, and the latter's wife Mary. James took refuge in France. A year later (4 April 1689), the Scottish Convention of Estates offered the new English monarchs the Scottish crown, which they accepted on 11 May 1689. In Scotland, those loyal to James resisted the ascendancy of William III and Mary II. Sir John Graham of Claverhouse, Viscount Dundee (known as both Bonnie Dundee and Bloody Clavers), who had been a member of the opposition minority at the Convention, helped to raise a Jacobite army with the aim of restoring the crown to James. In May of 1689, Dundee made his way to the Highlands to raise the clans. On 11 May 1689, Dundee entered Perth with a cavalry unit made up of his own Royal Regiment of Horse and local volunteers - *Taking of Perth* (11 May 1689). The only resistance, a newly-levied militia raised by the Laird of Blair, was easily defeated. A team of government tax collectors was captured by the Jacobites at Perth and their seized tax revenue ensured the Jacobite war chest could meet the immediate needs of its army. The western clans came under Viscount Dundee's command on 18 May at a spot close to the River Lochy. Despite appeals to James, only 300 to 400 Irish troops (led by Colonel Alexander Cannon) were sent to join his rising. The next few months were very difficult for the rebels who struggled to maintain their numbers and cohesion. Meanwhile, William ordered the Scottish government to assemble an army to crush the Jacobites. A large force of regulars (this army was almost entirely Scottish, having in its ranks only one English regiment) was placed under the command of General Hugh Mackay of Scourie whose stated intention was to defeat Dundee before larger numbers of Irish troops arrived in Scotland. Both sides raced to the central Highlands. Dundee won the race and took the strategically important Blair Castle, but in so doing sacrificed the size of his army, since the clans were still drifting in. When intelligence reached Dundee of Mackay's intention of marching his army into the Highlands and attacking Blair Castle, he moved the Jacobite army to meet them. Dundee marched his Highlanders over the Drumochter Pass as Mackay organised his troops at Dunkeld. The two armies came face-to-face at a spot north-west of the Pass of Killiecrankie - ***Battle of Killiecrankie*** (27 July 1689).

THE BATTLE OF KILLIECRANKIE
27 JULY 1689

Jacobite Army of James II (VII of Scotland)
c.2500 infantry
40 cavalry

Sir John MacLean's Regiment: (MacLeans) 200-300
Colonel Alexander Cannon's Irish Regiment: 300-400
Clan Ranald's MacDonalds: 480-600
Glengarry's MacDonalds: 200-300
Sir Ewan Cameron of Lochiel's Regiment: (Camerons: 240-500
Sir Alan MacLean of Duart's Regiment:
(MacLeans with a couple of companies of Irish regulars) 200
Sir Donald MacDonald of Sleat's Regiment: 400-500
Sir William Wallace of Craigie's Troop of Horse:
(16 under the Earl of Dunfermline) 40
Small independent groups of Athollmen

Notes
The cavalry units comprised men from Dundee's
Royal Regiment of Horse supplemented by volunteers.
The Jacobite infantry was in the main an inexperienced force
lacking in muskets and combat training.
Typical Highland weaponry included the 18-inch dirk, the
basket-hilted broadsword and targe (a leather-covered wooden shield).

Government Army of William of Orange
3500-4600 infantry and fusiliers
100-110 cavalry

Lieutenant Colonel George Lauder's mixed advance group: 200
Brigadier Bartholomew Balfour's Regiment - an element of the
Scots (Dutch) Brigade: (commanded by Major James Fergusson) 400-660
Brigadier George Ramsay's Regiment - an element of the
Scots (Dutch) Brigade: 400-660
General Hugh Mackay's Regiment - an element of the
Scots (Dutch) Brigade: (commanded by Mackay's younger brother,
Lieutenant Colonel James Mackay) 550-600
Alexander Viscount Kenmore's Regiment: 500-770
David Melville, 3rd Earl of Leven's Regiment: 600-870
Colonel Ferdinando Hastings' Regiment (English troops) - later the
13th Regiment of Foot: 600-850

A small group of sharpshooters (Highlanders) on the government right
operating as an independent company:
(commanded by Captain Robert Menzies of Weem) 80

Lord Belhaven's troop of cavalry: (militia) 60
Earl of Annandale's troop of cavalry: (militia) 50

3-9 small pieces of artillery (leather guns)
(under Master Gunner James Smith)

Notes
The Scots (Dutch) Brigade comprised professional soldiers
that formed a brigade of the Dutch Army.
The main regimental formations included grenadier companies
within their ranks.
Alexander Viscount Kenmore's Regiment were
inexperienced troops with little real combat experience.
Lieutenant Colonel George Lauder's mixed advance group
were in the main fusiliers armed with flintlocks.
Colonel Ferdinando Hastings' Regiment and David Melville,
3rd Earl of Leven's Regiment were both made up of veteran troops.
Infantry companies were armed with muskets or flintlocks
(two-thirds of each company) and pikemen - 15 foot pikes -
(one-third of each company).
The leather guns were manufactured by stiffening a central iron
barrel with splints around which was tightly wound iron wire and rope.
An outer leather wrapping protected further layers of canvas and timber.

THE BATTLE STORY

T HE JACOBITE ARMY reached Killiecrankie Pass first. Dundee deployed his men on the slope of a hill above the pass and awaited the government troops. A unit of Lochiel's Regiment was sent to occupy a small cottage that stood above Urrard House. Aware of his inferiority in numbers and arms, Dundee attempted to overcome these difficulties by the advantage of terrain.

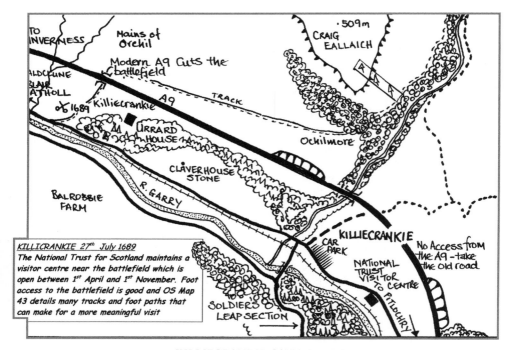

KILLIECRANKIE BATTLEFIELD.

As Mackay led his army from Dunkeld, Lieutenant Colonel Lauder's advance force of 200 men scouted along Killiecrankie Pass. Satisfied that the route was clear, Lauder placed his men in a birch wood at one end of the pass. By noon, the government army had passed by Moulin and its front sections were at the pass. Progress through the densely vegetated two-mile long track that ran along Killiecrankie Pass proved slow. It took four hours for the army to reach the other end. As the army marched through the pass, a local Athollman, Iain Macrae, tracked their movement from the safety of the western edge of the River Garry. Close to the present day railway viaduct, in a spot now named Trooper's Well, Macrae fired at and killed a government cavalry officer. Apart from this one incident, no signs of the Jacobite army were seen until the government troops reached the far end of the pass. At this point, the government vanguard mistook the movements of small groups of irregular Jacobite units as the leading section of Dundee's army. Their mistake was soon realised, when the entire Jacobite army was spotted in battle formation above the pass floor and along the steep slopes of the mouth of the pass. Despite his weaker position, Mackay felt that his greater numbers and better-quality cavalry would give him victory and so he deployed his men for battle. The government army was arranged along a narrow terrace; this ran in a north-east direction (parallel to the modern A9 road). His army stood just in front of Urrard House with the River Garry behind hampering any potential retreat.

Mackay placed his two cavalry units in the centre to give them room to manoeuvre. He protected his right wing by anchoring adjacent to a stream and deploying Menzies' unit of sharpshooters, whilst Lauder's mixed unit secured the left by digging into the forested rise above Aldclune. The left wing was placed under the command of Brigadier Balfour who was second-in-command of the government army. To increase his frontage, Mackay thinned out sections of his line: Leven's Regiment, the government army's strongest formation operated three ranks deep whilst its weakest formation, Kenmore's Regiment, maintained a standard six ranks. The increased frontage allowed the government army to train more weapons on the ground across which the expected Highland Charge would come, but it also meant that it had no reserve. Mackay's problems were further compounded by the existence of a bog between his left and centre and by the wide space between Ramsay's and Kenmore's regiments; the distance between these two regiments was too large to allow effective musket coverage and left Kenmore's inexperienced soldiers isolated.

Across the pass, Dundee had his own set of problems. His

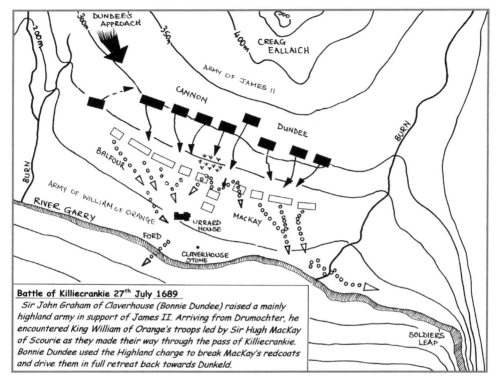

Battle of Killiecrankie 27th July 1689
Sir John Graham of Claverhouse (Bonnie Dundee) raised a mainly highland army in support of James II. Arriving from Drumochter, he encountered King William of Orange's troops led by Sir Hugh MacKay of Scourie as they made their way through the pass of Killiecrankie. Bonnie Dundee used the Highland charge to break MacKay's redcoats and drive them in full retreat back towards Dunkeld.

BATTLE OF KILLIECRANKIE.

centre was secured by his best troops, but his wings were weak. The advantage of the slopes for the Highland Charge was also a disadvantage for his horse who might find it difficult to manoeuvre and operate effectively.

For over two hours, the two opposing armies stared at each other. The first move could only come from Dundee who had the advantage of the heights. During the stand-off, ineffective musket fire punctuated the wait. The government cannon proved just as useless. Not only did they fail to have the range to inflict damage, two of the gun carriages snapped after only a few rounds of firing. The only significant action at this point took place around some cottages lower down the slopes. In this fire-fight, Mackay's men bested a section of Lochiel's unit.

As the evening light began to fail - around 7.30pm - the Jacobites attacked. About 50 paces from the government line, the Jacobite regiments discharged a round and then came on with dirk, claymore and musket butt. The depth of the Jacobite attack was far deeper than the government defensive line. Intensive fire from Mackay's troops felled some 600 Jacobites in the first wave. The Jacobite charge continued against Mackay's centre where the regiments of Kenmore and Leven took the brunt of the attack. Lochiel mistakenly took his Camerons across the fire-zone of Leven's troops and his losses were severe. At this point, the government soldiers attempted to fix their new screw-in plug bayonets with which they had been equipped. This proved not only difficult due to a design fault, but also meant that their muskets ceased firing. Before long, hand-to-hand fighting had begun in the centre. Mackay's decision to thin his line, though effective against the charging Jacobites, now proved a disaster as the Highlanders poured into their over-stretched line in depth. A section of the government army turned, broke and ran, pursued by the Jacobites; their flight took them through the location of their baggage train. This turned out to be fortuitous for them as the presence of the baggage and supplies diverted many of the Jacobites who broke off their pursuit in order to plunder the government supplies. Only Mackay's Regiment, half of Leven's Regiment and a fraction of Hastings' Regiment remained in position.

During the attack, Mackay sent in his cavalry against the Jacobite infantry, but despite their superiority of numbers, Dundee's cavalry drove off the government horse. As the government cavalry made their way back to their lines, they disrupted the firing of their own troops. The Highlanders took advantage of this and very soon captured the government cannon.

The Jacobite attention now focussed on Mackay's Regiment which, despite decimating Lochiel's unit, soon broke. A small group of

GOVERNMENT REDCOAT AT KILLIECRANKIE.

soldiers with Lieutenant Colonel James Mackay stood its ground as the bulk of the regiment fled. They were all killed.

Precise firing from the government right saved the day from being a complete rout. Up to a sixth of Jacobite losses were men picked off by accurate firing from this part of the government army. On the government left, Brigadier Balfour struggled to make sense of the battle. Seeing the carnage inflicted in the centre and believing the day to be lost, he ordered the retreat. Balfour's withdrawal from the field proved difficult due to the terrain and his men became easy targets for the Athollmen and MacLean's Regiment who pursued them. Just as he neared Aldclune, Balfour himself was cornered by some Highlanders and, after refusing to surrender, was slain. Elsewhere, Ramsay's men had similar problems as they attempted to escape across the River Garry. Less than half of that regiment reached the safety of the far side of the river. It might have been a similar tale for Mackay's Regiment had not effective government musket fire delayed the Highlanders pursuit of their foe. Wallace's Horse managed to swing wide enough around the fire-zone to harry the retreating government infantry. Mackay's fleeing troops did not stop until they had reached the safety of Stirling Castle; 400 of them made it to Stirling.

In the ensuing mêlée, General Mackay was left alone on the battlefield now deserted by the Jacobites. He soon located elements of his army - the remaining half of Leven's Regiment and parts of his own and Kenmore's Regiment. To his right, Hastings' Regiment had survived an attack by Sleat's MacDonalds, killing not only many of Sleat's soldiers but Sir Donald MacDonald as well. Mackay proceeded to organise his remaining forces. As he deployed the rump of his army into a better location, he became aware of the Jacobite regiments re-grouping for a renewed attack. He was at this stage unaware that Viscount Dundee had been mortally wounded during the fighting. The government army commander issued orders for the retreat over the adjacent hill and onto Drummond Castle. The fight now over, the Highlanders completed the looting of the government baggage train. Mackay was disgusted by the performance of many of his troops and, after the battle, was recorded as saying that most of his men had behaved *"like the vilest cowards in nature".*

Viscount Dundee was a conspicuous target in the battle, clothed as he was in a silver and buff coat dressed with a green scarf. Always a frontline leader, Dundee charged with his cavalry against Hastings' Regiment. Sharpshooters easily picked him off. The body of Dundee was taken from the field and buried in the churchyard at Old Blair; he was only 41 years of age. There is a monument to him in that now-ruined kirkyard.

Estimates of the casualty levels for the government army range from 1000 to 1250 dead and about 500 men captured. Jacobite losses were as high, with around 1200 dead. On one level, the Jacobite performance at Killiecrankie was a great victory for the rebels. However, on the important level of motivation and leadership, the loss of Dundee at that moment of the rising signalled the end. On the government side, Mackay soon recovered from his defeat and immediately began organising for the battles ahead.

The site of the Battle of Killiecrankie lies principally on private agricultural land sliced across by the A9 bypass and a railway line. The National Trust for Scotland's Killiecrankie Visitor Centre (opened in 1964) is located on the south-eastern fringes of the battlefield and includes the Soldier's Leap. The Leap is the spot where a government soldier, Donald MacBean, is alleged to have escaped from pursuing Highlanders by jumping the 18-foot gap across the River Garry. There are several stones and features at Killiecrankie associated with the battle.

The Claverhouse Stone, which lies south-west of the battle site in a flat field, is traditionally thought to be where Viscount Dundee met his death. However, the unmarked stone, 4 ft-5 ft high, is an ancient one that pre-dates the battle and there is no conclusive evidence to justify its name; it is probably Pictish and is located close to where the government baggage was placed during the battle.

Trenches constructed by the Jacobite army to secure its position are still visible on the battlefield to this day.

The Balfour Stone is located halfway along Killiecrankie Pass. It bears the inscription:

> *Here Brigadier Balfour of the Dutch Brigade, who commanded the left wing of General Mackay's army, was killed in the subsequent rout by the Atholl men.*

Another monument to the battle, Mount (Tomb) Clavers is normally considered the site of a mass grave of officers and is marked by a plaque. Like the Claverhouse Stone, there is no evidence to support this tradition; it is most likely a cenotaph. Upon this stone, there is another plaque - dated 1950 - with the inscription:

Ian Campbell Younger of Urrard, killed in Malaya - 24.

Recent archaeological work at Killiecrankie has yielded a great deal of material from the battle, including lead bullets, a grenade fragment and uniform buttons.

The memoirs of General Mackay include a reference to a minor battle between government forces and about 200 Athollmen that took place after the Battle of Killiecrankie: *"At St. Johnston we surprised a party of a couple of hundred men, whereof 150 were killed."* Those Highlanders involved with the **Surprise at Perth** (July/August 1689) were most likely newly-arrived recruits to King James' Standard; after Killiecrankie, the Jacobite Army ranks were swollen by new troop arrivals such as the Stewarts of Appin. With the death of Viscount Dundee, the command of the Jacobite troops fell to Colonel Cannon. He marched his replenished army along the River Tay towards Dunkeld.

This small settlement, less than 20 miles from Perth was secured for the government by a small garrison: Lieutenant Colonel William Cleland's Cameronian Regiment (26th Regiment of Foot).

Cleland was a veteran soldier. Despite only being 28 years of age, he had been a key figure in the defeat of Dundee at Drumclog (1 June 1679) and had fought at Bothwell Brig (22 June 1679). The Cameronians had been formed by the Earl of Angus only four months prior to the **Battle of Dunkeld** (21 August 1689) and were comprised of soldiers from a highly religious Lowland Puritan sect. The regiment drew its name from the

CLELAND'S TROOPS HOLD THE JACOBITES AT DUNKELD CATHEDRAL.

Covenanter martyr Richard Cameron. The Cameronians entered Dunkeld on 17 August 1689. A day later, two troops of horse and three troops of dragoons (led by Lord Cardross) joined Cleland's Regiment at Dunkeld. Within days of the garrisoning of Dunkeld, minor skirmishes occurred outside the town between government and Jacobite patrols. That same day, the military commander at Perth, Colonel Ramsay, made a decision to reinforce Perth and so Lord Cardross' cavalry and dragoons were redeployed south. His force reduced, Cleland fortified Dunkeld and dug in his troops as best he could. Dunkeld was not a walled town and so the Cameronians built trenches and reinforced the low garden dykes around the Marquis of Atholl's mansion (which lay north of Dunkeld Cathedral) and around the cathedral. The cathedral and mansion were designated the final redoubt for the battle. A small unit of musketeers was placed high up in the cathedral tower.

THE BATTLE OF DUNKELD
21 AUGUST 1689

Jacobite Army of James II (VII of Scotland)
c.5000 troops (infantry and cavalry)
4 troops of horse
A small amount of artillery

Government Army of William of Orange
700-1200 infantry

THE BATTLE STORY

AT 7AM ON 21 AUGUST 1689 (a Wednesday) Jacobite infantry, supported by four troops of horse, moved against the surrounded garrison at Dunkeld. The town was attacked from the south-west and north-east simultaneously but despite the overwhelming numerical superiority of the Jacobites, progress through the town was costly in both time and lives. Every street and house became a hand-to-hand battle and as the Cameronians retreated, they fired the vacated houses and moved more and more men into the cathedral and mansion house where their final stand had been planned.

Lieutenant Colonel Cleland perished in the early stages of the battle, taking a bullet to the head and another to the liver. His second-in-command, Major Henderson, also died in the battle. The garrison command then fell to Captain George Munro of Auchinbowie.

Wave after wave of Jacobite attacks against the Cameronian defensive positions ended in failure. Many Jacobite soldiers occupying positions in houses around the cathedral were burned to death as small commando raiding groups of Cameronians fired the buildings with burning faggots held on the end of pikes. Constructed of wood, heather and turf the houses burned so quickly that Jacobite musketeers firing from upper floors were unable to escape the flames. The defenders made good use of the roof of the Atholl mansion, stripping the lead to manufacture musket rounds in small furrows in the ground.

For fours hours the Battle of Dunkeld raged. It ended only after 300 Jacobite soldiers and 50 Cameronians lay dead in the town's streets. Around noon, despite the protestation of their officers, the Jacobites stopped fighting and left the town. Only three houses remained standing in Dunkeld and today the town is almost entirely made up of buildings constructed after 1689.

The Battle of Dunkeld is remembered in a Jacobite ballad that lays testament to the fighting prowess of Cleland's troops:

> *You fought like devils, your only rivals,*
> *When you were at Dunkeld, boys.*

Cleland is buried in the nave of Dunkeld Cathedral, below the tower. In a twist of irony, he lies near a Colonel Rohenstart of Rohenstart (died 1854) who was the last descendent of Prince Charles Edward Stewart.

The Jacobite rebellion in Scotland lasted another year before it was crushed on 1 May 1690 when six troops of dragoons under Sir Thomas Livingstone (commander of the Inverness garrison) surprised the Jacobite Army in a dawn raid at its camp at the Haughs of Cromdale near Grantown-on-Spey (Battle of Cromdale 30 April-1 May 1690). In this battle over 400 Jacobite soldiers were captured. General Mackay built forts across the Highlands, at Fort William and elsewhere, as a means to subjugate the Jacobites. On 1 July 1690,

James II (VII of Scotland) was completely defeated by William of Orange at the Battle of the Boyne in Ireland.

Queen Anne came to the throne in 1702. Five years later the Acts of Union were established. These acts were very unpopular in many parts of Scotland and further Jacobite unrest followed. The first, the invasion of 1708, involving French ships and 6000 soldiers, was a complete failure from the very start; the troops did not even set foot in Scotland. A more significant rising followed the death of Queen Anne and the crowning of George I, the Elector of Hanover. John Erskine, the 6th Earl of Mar was sacked as Secretary of State by the newly-crowned George I. Mar then raised the Jacobite standard at Braemar on 6 September 1715. Jacobite risings began in three parts of the Union: south-west England, Galloway and the Borders, and in the Highlands. Mar's plan was to bring his Highlanders down to unite with the other areas of Jacobite resistance. Inverness was taken easily but Edinburgh remained under government control. Colonel John Hay of Cromlix, the eldest son of the Earl of Kinnoull, took Perth without battle on 14 September. With only 40 horsemen at his disposal, Hay succeeded in fooling the town's defenders into surrender - **Capture of Perth** (14 September 1715). The town now became a rallying point for the Jacobite clans, so that by 24 September, Mar stood at Perth with an estimated 10000 troops. This force was supplemented by men under the command of General Gordon at Auchterarder. Although sizeable in number, the Jacobite army lacked combat skill. Nevertheless, had Mar immediately sent his men into the field, he might have taken the whole of Scotland for his king. Instead, he wasted valuable time at Perth and allowed the government to organise its response to the rebellion.

SALUTATION HOTEL, PERTH,
DATING FROM 1699.

Whilst at Perth, the Jacobite army command billeted at the Salutation Hotel. (Thirty years later, during the '45, Bonnie Prince Charlie also used the Salutation Hotel.) The town was fortified and plans were drawn up for the construction of a major defensive citadel. The majority of Perth residents in 1715 were pro-Jacobite and Mar's troops enjoyed the support of the local people during their few months of occupancy.

John Campbell, 2nd Duke of Argyll, the commander-in-chief of George I's army in Scotland stood at Stirling with a Hanoverian army of only 3000 men. This army was made up of regular Scottish and English regiments as well local militia units commanded by General Joseph Wightman. The Duke of Argyll was a highly competent military leader who had served under the Duke of Marlborough in the War of the Spanish Succession.

On 10 November 1715, Mar took his army, arranged into four divisions, out of Perth. His infantry camped at Auchterarder and his cavalry at Dunning. At this point, he suffered losses from his ranks when Clan Fraser was ordered to leave by its leader. General Gordon was ordered to move ahead and secure Dunblane, but Argyll, aware of this intention, succeeded in occupying the town first - Sunday 12 November. Mar's plan was to avoid Argyll and move south by crossing the Forth. Informed by General Gordon as to Argyll's position at Dunblane, Mar made the decision to meet the Hanoverian army in the field.

Argyll placed his force a few miles from Dunblane, around Kippenross House. Many of his officers knew this area and Argyll felt that would be to his advantage. Mar took his army towards Dunblane, making camp on the moorland of Kinbuck. This position allowed him to control the route to Dunblane. The **Battle of Sheriffmuir** (13 November 1715) - originally known as the Battle of Dunblane - took place the next day. First to arrive at Sheriffmuir, Mar chose his ground carefully. He protected his left by a bog near a burn, placed his left wing under his most experienced officer, General Hamilton, and positioned himself on his army's right. Unbeknown to Mar, an overnight freeze had left the bog hard and his left vulnerable to a flanking attack.

The Hanoverian army marched out of Dunblane. Much smaller than its enemy, it nevertheless had the advantage of large numbers of cavalry. Argyll and his officer corps climbed a ridge near Stonehill Farm (south-east of Dunblane) and spied down upon the Jacobite regiments. Reaching Sheriffmuir, he deployed his cavalry on the right, placed Wightman's militia in the centre and Lieutenant General Whitham's cavalry on the left. As the two armies deployed on the moor, the citizens of Dunblane watched the battle from Lady's Mount (close to the Queen Victoria School in Dunblane).

BATTLE OF SHERIFFMUIR
13 NOVEMBER 1715

Jacobite Army of James II (VII of Scotland)
8000-12000
at least 6200-6290 infantry
807-900 horse

Marquis of Huntly's Squadron (horse)
Stirlingshire (Linlithgow's) Squadron (horse) - with the Royal Standard
Perthshire (Rollo's) Squadron (horse)
Fifeshire Squadron (horse)

Some ten battalions of Highland clansmen [including those of
MacDonald, Glengarry; Breadalbane, Clan Ranald and MacLean] (foot)
(commander General Gordon)
Earl of Marischal's two squadrons (horse)
Earl of Seaforth's two battalions (foot)
Lord Huntly's two battalions (foot)
Earl Panmure's Battalion (foot)
Marquis of Tullibardine's Battalion (foot)
Drummond's and Viscount Strathallan's two battalions (foot)
Struan's (Strowan's) Battalion (foot)
Angus (Southesk's) Squadron (horse)
A reserve battalion of 800 men (foot)

Hanoverian Army of George I
3000-4000 - most likely 3400-3500
8 regiments (2200) infantry
5 regiments (960) dragoons

Carpenter's Dragoons: (horse) 180
Colonel Kerr's Dragoons: (horse) 180
Six battalions of regulars:
Brigadier Lord Forfar's: (foot) 320
Major General Wightman's: (foot) 250
Lord Shannon's: (foot) 340
Morrison's: (foot) 240
Montague's: (foot) 240
Brigadier Clayton's: (foot) 240

Scots Greys (Portmore's): (horse) 180
Lieutenant General Evan's Dragoons: (horse) 180
Troop of about 60 volunteers: (horse)
Edgerton's Battalions: (foot) 250
Orrery's Battalion: (foot) 320
E. Stair's two troops of dragoons: (horse) 180

Notes
The Scots Greys were the Royal Regiment of North British Dragoons.
Lieutenant General Whitham and Brigadier Grant commanded on the left.
Major General Wightman and Brigadier Clayton commanded in the centre.
Lieutenant General Evans and Brigadier Lord Forfar
commanded on the right.
Argyll led from the right.

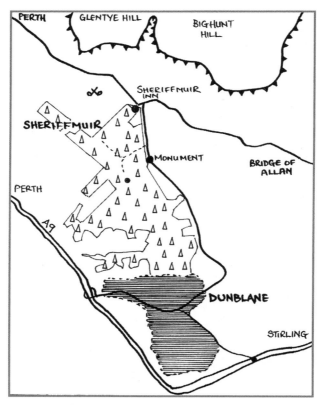

SHERIFFMUIR BATTLEFIELD.

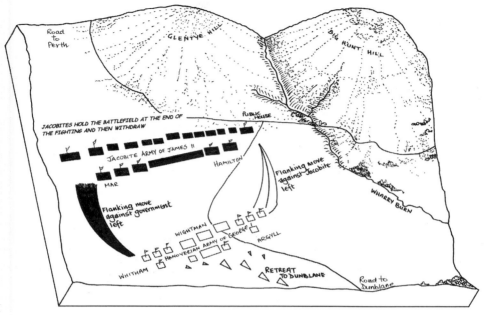

BATTLE OF SHERIFFMUIR.

THE BATTLE STORY

TO THE SOUND of their drums, the government army prepared to advance. Before they could organise correctly for the advance, the MacLeans attacked the government's left. This attack was supported by troops from the Jacobite centre. In no time, this entire wing broke under the Highland onslaught. General Whitham and his troops left the field and did not stop until they reached Stirling.

On the government right things were very different. The Jacobite charge was met head on by Argyll's best troops who managed to repel the attackers. The Jacobites made major blunders on their left when advancing troop units were mixed up and ended up either in the centre or on the right. This seriously weakened their left wing. Argyll himself now led the counter-attack with about 1500 men, both infantry and cavalry. Aided by the frozen bog, the government horse moved around to flank the Jacobites and came crashing into their lines. This might have immediately broken the entire Jacobite left had not a stand been made by the Fife and Angus units. As the Scots Greys made easy work of their opposition, and as Evan's Dragoons made headway, the rout could not be held off for very long. Seaforth's infantry battalions took very heavy casualties and they, along with the other Jacobite units, broke. The rout of the Jacobite left continued all the way to the River Allan some two to three miles from the battlefield. At various points in their three-hour flight, sections of the Jacobite army attempted to rally and several stands were made, but to no avail.

Oblivious to the fate of the rest of his army, Argyll pushed his men on to pursue the fleeing rebels. When eventually he rode back to the battlefield with a thousand horse, he became aware of the destruction of his entire left wing. Despite the success against the Jacobite left, the government army was still the weaker of the two forces in both numbers and position. Quickly, Argyll set about organising a defensive arrangement on Kippendavie Hill by building mud walls and other enclosures. At this point, he had about 2000 troops at his disposal. Mar now ordered his army to attack the government position. This attack failed to breach Argyll's defences and, as the light faded, the Jacobite army sounded the retreat.

Mar marched his army to Ardoch, then the following morning back to Sheriffmuir to claim the field (and the victory) before falling back to Perth while Argyll retreated into Dunblane to reorganise his troops. Seven regiments of horse and twelve of foot soon reinforced the government army. The battle losses on both sides were extensive. The Jacobite army lost about 600-800 killed, 100 captured, 4 cannon and 13 or 14 colours. Amongst the Jacobite dead was Alan Dearg MacDonald of Clan Ranald whose dying body was taken from Sheriffmuir to Drummond Castle. He is buried at Innerpeffray Chapel. On the government side, the dead amounted to 290-320. In addition, 114-187 men were wounded, 100-133 taken prisoner, 1400 arms were lost and 4 colours were captured.

The site of the Battle of Sheriffmuir is today almost entirely owned by the Forestry Commission. The easiest way to visit the battle site is by the A9 road. Three monuments connected with the battle are visible to visitors to Sheriffmuir.

There is a tall structure, raised in 1915, to Clan Macrae. Upon this monument is written:

> *In memory of the Macraes killed at Sheriffmuir 13 November 1715 when defending the Royal House of Stuart. The Kintail and Lochalsh companies formed part of the left wing of the army and fell almost to a man.*

Adjacent to the Clan Macrae memorial is a small cairn erected in recent times by the 1745 Association. It bears the inscription:

> *On this moor on 13 November 1715, a Jacobite army composed largely of Highlanders under the command of the Earl of Mar met a Hanoverian army consisting mainly of regular British soldiers under the Duke of Argyll, at which became known as the Battle of Sheriffmuir. The result was indecisive, but Mar's failure to take advantage of Argyll's weakened position in the closing stages of the conflict and subsequent withdrawal from the field contributed to the failure of the Rising - known as 'The Fifteen' - in favour of the restoration of the exiled King James VII (the Old Chevalier).*

Four hundred metres from the Clan Macrae memorial, accessible by a footpath through a fir tree wood, is the Gathering Stone (also known as the Battle Stone, Beltane Stone, Carline's Stane or Gatherums' Stane) made from a block of grit. Since 1840 this low memorial has been protected from vandals and souvenir hunters by a series of iron hoops. The stone is considered as both the point where Argyll stood before the commencement of battle and where the clans raised their standards. Close to the Gathering Stone are several earth-mounds traditionally thought to be Jacobite graves.

The Jacobite army remained in Perth for the next few months until forced to leave at the end of January (1716) by the approach of Argyll's replenished force. To facilitate their retreat, Mar ordered his men to undertake raids across the Strathearn region - Aberuthven, Auchterarder, Blackford, Crieff, Dunning and Muthill - as a means of slowing down the march of the Hanoverian army. Only Comrie, a pro-Jacobite village was spared the torch by the raiders. After the Jacobite withdrawal from Perth, the town was garrisoned by government troops.

Raid on Aberuthven and Auchterarder - Auchterarder was set ablaze during a raid on Wednesday, 25 January at 4am.

Raid on Blackford - Two to three hundred Jacobite soldiers marched into Blackford on the evening of 25 January (between 9pm and 10pm) with the support of a small cavalry force. In undertaking the raid, the Jacobites were assisted by a local man, William Maitland (the son of James Maitland, a local innkeeper).

Burning of Crieff - On 26 January, a party of around 350 clansmen (MacDonalds and Camerons) entered Crieff and fired the town.

Burning of Dunning - Dunning was set ablaze at 5pm on 28 January 1716 by a contingent of Highlanders led by Lord George Murray. The firestorm created by the arson attack was so extreme that only one house, the Straw House, survived the flames. According to a traditional tale, the owner of that house, by employing burning damp straw, tricked Murray's men into believing that her house was already ablaze. A few months after the destruction of their town the people of Dunning erected a thorn tree as a memorial. This tree flourished until 1936 when it was felled by a fierce storm. The present memorial tree in Dunning's Thorntree Square is the fourth tree planted since 1716.

Burning of Muthill - Around about 8pm or 9pm on 28 January a small force (50) of MacDonalds, MacLeans and Camerons led by a Captain of Clan Ranald entered Muthill and set the town on fire.

The Battle of Sheriffmuir was a rather strange affair when viewed with hindsight. Both sides declared themselves the victor, both sides outflanked and destroyed their enemy's left and both generals' performance was lacking. Mar and Argyll were criticised after the battle for failing to utilise all the troops available to them, instead concentrating on using only one wing of their respective armies. Ultimately, the government was the real victor at Sheriffmuir. Jacobite army casualties, serious desertion levels and subsequent recruitment and morale difficulties meant that the 1715 rising, like those before it, was once again doomed to failure. Even when James III (VIII of Scotland) himself landed in Scotland to lead his army, insufficient troops for his cause could be mustered. After a brief visit to Perth on 9 January 1716, James left the following month for exile in France, where he was joined by the Earl of Mar. James' dreams of retaining the Scottish crown were at an end. Those surviving Jacobite troops that had rallied to their king's standard returned to their homes. Four years later, in 1719, another rising - the Little Rising - this time with the assistance of the Spanish state, also ended in disappointment.

On 25 July 1745, Charles Edward Stuart landed at Moidart on Scotland's west coast, signalling the start of the final Jacobite rising. A month later (19 August 1745), Bonnie Prince Charlie raised the Stuart standard at Glenfinnan. With 1000 men under his command, Charles then moved eastwards to Crieff and Blair Castle before entering Perth with 200 troops under the command of the Duke of Perth; the Jacobite army was under the joint control of two Lieutenant Generals, the Duke of Perth and Lord George Murray. The Prince Regent's entrance into Perth took him past the North Port, Castle Gable, Skinnergate and down the High Street. As he progressed through the town, the bells of St. John's Kirk, commandeered by a local Jacobite supporter (one of the town's barbers), rang out in salute. *Occupation of Perth* (3 September 1745).

Like his father before him, Charles occupied a room at the Salutation Hotel - Room 12 - where he received visitors and planned his tactics over the next eight days. Lieutenant General Murray spent his time at Perth drilling the slowly growing Jacobite army on Perth's North Inch. On the Atholl Street side of the North Inch there is a memorial plaque which recalls the mustering of Jacobite troops on that inch.

The Mercat Cross in Perth was the scene for a ceremonial declaration of James III (VIII of Scotland) as king of Scotland. The day after the Jacobite entry into Perth, Clan Ranald and Keppoch led a small force of MacDonalds through the Carse of Gowrie to Dundee where two government supply ships were seized. This raid yielded vital supplies of arms and ammunition for the Jacobite cause.

When the main Jacobite force left Perth for Edinburgh on 11 September they numbered 2400 men; the town was left under the authority of the Laird of Gask and a small garrison. By 1 November 1745, the Jacobite army was on the march southwards towards England. After their return from Derby and the subsequent loss of both Edinburgh and Stirling, Perth became the assembly point of the volunteers loyal to the House of Stuart.

Of note during the rising were two military events:

Sack of Bunrannoch (1745) - This now deserted village that dates back to the middle ages was raided, sacked and burned to the ground by Jacobite troops during the 1745 rising.

Siege of Blair Castle (1745-6) - Blair Castle was placed under siege twice during the '45, the first time by the Jacobites under Lord George Murray and subsequently by government troops in early 1746.

A government army was defeated at Falkirk on 17 January 1746. Nevertheless, after an aborted attack on Stirling Castle, the Jacobite army began to retreat to the north of Scotland. At Crieff on 1 February 1746, the Jacobite army split into two divisions. The first division of the Highland clans travelled north to Inverness with Prince Charles. The second, that of

Lord George Murray and comprising cavalry, Lowland infantry and about 100 French soldiers, made tracks for Perth. Murray's vanguard reached Perth at 7pm on Sunday 2 February. It took over five hours for the 20 tail-end ammunition carts to get to the relative safety of the town. Jacobite stragglers were still coming into Perth the next day. The respite at Perth was very short. By the following Tuesday, as the Duke of Cumberland approached Perth with over 10000 men, the Jacobites were on the move again. To increase their speed of retreat, huge quantities of supplies and heavy weaponry were abandoned. Thirty cannon and 13 field guns (8-pounders and 12-pounders) were spiked to be made unusable. Fourteen swivel guns were pushed into the River Tay along with a large quantity of cannon balls. These guns were enormous devices weighing one-and-three-quarter tons, each requiring a team of 20 horses. A large stockpile of gunpowder stored in Perth's Tollbooth was sold to a local merchant. Within the Tollbooth were several prisoners-of-war who were released as the Jacobite division pulled out of Perth on Tuesday 4 February.

The Jacobite retreat took them through Coupar Angus and then northwards. Luckily for the fleeing army the weather was extremely bad and this slowed down their pursuers. Perth returned to government control on 4 February and, for a short time, 5000 Hanoverian troops camped on the North Inch. The administration of the town's affairs was placed in the hands of a junta who set up a Court of Inquisition. Across Perthshire, Jacobite supporters were arrested and hauled before the military court; their property was seized and sold at auction in Perth. Amongst the notable arrestees were Viscountess Strathallan and the Duchess of Perth.

On 16 April 1746, the final battle of the 1745 rising took place at Culloden. This defeat of the Jacobites was the end of the House of Stuart's cause. The aftermath of the battle was bloody and brutal: the Highland clans were persecuted and their way of life proscribed. After being pursued for some time, Charles Edward Stuart made his way to France and then onto Rome, never to be king.

CHAPTER 5

TWO CENTURIES OF CLAN WARFARE

THE HIGHLANDS OF PERTHSHIRE, being as they are well suited for cattle grazing, were in the past easy prey for the rustling of said beasts. In the majority of cases of cattle theft the motivating factor was financial, but in some, the desire to extend power and influence over the territory of a rival clan was at the fore. A case in point is the raid co-ordinated by Duncan Stewart, son of Alexander Stewart, the Wolf of Badenoch - *Raid of Angus and Kinloch* and the *Running Skirmish at Glasclune* - Water of Isla - (1389 or August 1392). This was the culmination of a long-running dispute concerned with issues of land, inheritance and power. Three hundred men of Atholl and Badenoch joined Duncan Stewart in the raid: Donnachies, Fergussons, and Chattans. Robert of Atholl, head of Clan Donnachie, brought his men on the raid to seek revenge on Alexander Lindsay whose wife had received an inheritance which Robert of Atholl deemed due to his spouse.

The raiding party travelled across Angus, stealing cattle, firing houses and killing anyone that opposed them. Over 3000 cows were taken and several Lindsays and Ogilvys were murdered. The rustled cattle were slowly driven westwards. As the cattle and raiders entered the valley of Lornty (Blairgowrie), north of Glasclune, a force of men assembled from Glen Isla, Glenshee, Glen Esk and Lowland Perthshire attacked them. The battle was a running skirmish over many miles, beginning initially at Balmacaan (by Dalnavaid Bridge), continuing onto Dail-Chosnaidh (field of contending) and then concluding at Clais-chatha (pass of battle or battle hollow). Eventually, the men of Angus withdrew having been thoroughly beaten.

Not deterred by their initial losses at Glasclune the survivors, after obtaining reinforcements, pursued their foe into Strathardle and the land of the Donnachies. Alerted as to the presence of armed men on their land, Clan Donnachie prepared for battle. Despite being joined by Sir Walter Ogilvy (Sheriff of Angus), Sir Patrick Gray, Sir David Lindsay and 60 armed men, the men of Angus were defeated once more.

To counter the superior manoeuvrability of the mounted men-at-arms, Duncan Stewart chose to fight on ground unsuited to horses. About six miles from Pitlochry, at Glen Brierachan, a second battle ensued. In the fighting, Sir Walter Ogilvy's half-brother Leighton (Laird of Ulishaven), the Lairds of Auchterlony, Cairncross, Guthrie and Forfar and some 50 to 60 other men were killed. There is a popular account of the death of Lindsay. The story recounts that Lindsay, having captured a raider and pinned him to the ground with his lance, was then grievously wounded by the same man, who just before he expired, succeeded in pulling himself up the lance and with a swing of his claymore, cut through his captor's leg down to the bone.

Soon after the raid, the legal authorities began procedures against Clan Donnachie and their allies. Duncan and Robert Stewart, as well as Thomas and Robert Atholl were decreed outlaws. In 1392, an act of forfeiture was enacted against the Donnachies.

Probably the most famous of all the battles to have taken place in Perthshire is that immortalised by Sir Walter Scott in his *Fair Maid of Perth* as the **Battle of the Clans** (28 September 1396). Two clans, Clan Chattan and Clan Quhele (Kay or MacKay or Cameron), agreed to settle a long-standing feud, likely linked to the Raid on Angus, under Scone Abbey's right of judicial combat. The contest, organised by the High Constable, the Baron of Errol (a member of the Hay family) and Sir David Lindsay, took place on Perth's North Inch. A wooden stockade was constructed on the inch and 30 men from each clan entered the arena to fight to the death. Scotland's monarch, Robert III, viewed the gladia-torial battle with his queen, Anabella Drummond, from a *'Gilten Arbor'* situated where Atholl Place is today. Victory went to Clan Chattan. Of the 30 men of Clan Quhele that entered the stockade, only one man survived and he was forced to

CLAN WARRIOR.

swim the River Tay to escape. Clan Chattan's losses amounted to 10 dead. There is a memorial on the Atholl Street side of the North Inch that commemorates the battle. On Saturday 24 September 1932, the Boy Scouts of Perth and County ended a pageant through the town with a re-enactment of this famous episode in Perth's history. The re-enactment formed part of the commemoration of the centenary of the death of Sir Walter Scott.

In Glen Lyon there is a large rock commonly known as the Stone of Sandals. Its name records a fierce battle between two rival clans - **Clan Battle of Glen Lyon** (c.1488). The dispute centred on land ownership and an associated murder. To attempt to settle the matter by agreement, Ivor Campbell brought his MacIvors to Glen Lyon to meet the Stewarts of Garth Castle under their commander Neil Stewart. After failing to resolve their differences, the two sides retired to prepare for battle. A traditional account of the fighting details how the Stewarts removed their sandals before battle and placed them on a large rock. It is said that by doing so, they would know their casualties as each unclaimed pair would signify a man lost.

The Stewarts made easy work of their enemy who were pursued and killed in flight over a distance of some eight miles. The MacIvors in an open field at Meggernie made a final stand. Here they perished to a man. Over 140 MacIvors lost their lives in that clan battle.

King James IV, displeased with the behaviour of both clans, stepped in to force Campbell and Stewart to sit down and end their conflict. The matter was settled in favour of Campbell on 15 October 1488.

Another clan feud that led to a violent confrontation was that between the Macnabs of Killin and Clan Neish of Loch Earn. Fought at Glen Boltachan (north of St. Fillans), near to Littleport Farm, around the end of the 15th century, the **Clan Battle of Glen Boltachan** (c.1490 or 1522) was won by the Macnabs. There is a sizeable boulder on the battle site believed to be where the Neish's clan chief was killed. Popular accounts tell of him being surrounded by Macnabs, many of whom he slew, before finally being brought down by overwhelming numbers. The red lichen that covers the granite boulders scattered around Glen Boltachan is said by locals to be stained by the blood of the fallen Neish clan chief. Living in fear of the Macnabs, Clan Neish relocated to a small island at the eastern end of Loch Earn, subsisting by means of thievery. One of their robbery expeditions was committed against the Macnabs and resulted in the murder of a servant. The Macnabs, swearing vengeance for this crime, plotted to deal with their old foe. A suitable boat was found and John Macnab, with 11 men, crossed Loch Tay and then Loch Earn (by Glentarken) to attack the Neish island homestead. Only one person survived the attack, a young boy; the rest of his clan were beheaded.

The farm at Dunan Rannoch was the site of a fight between Clan Eoin Buidhe and the Stewarts of Appin - **Fight at Dunan Rannoch** (15th century). In the battle, Clan Eoin Buidhe was almost wiped out. A small stream

(Caochan-na-Fola, the rill of blood) designates the battle site.

Inter-clan rivalry often led to alliances with other families in order to over-come a common enemy. At a small eminence of the River Earn's southern side, Cnoc-Mary (Knock Mary), two clans, the Murrays and the Drummonds, met in battle. Victory in this **Battle of Cnoc-Mary** (1490 or 1511) went to the Murrays, who returned home to Monzievaird with their spoils. The Drummonds, returning home with their dead and wounded, were met en route by a force of Campbells seeking retribution from the Murrays for the murder of Drummond of Monzie. Duncan Campbell of Dunstaffnage united his men with the surviving Drummonds and proceeded to Monzievaird.

Fearing the worst, the Murrays took refuge in the parish church of Monzievaird with their wives and children. The small thatched church was surrounded, but despite goading, the Murrays remained inside. Just as Duncan Campbell was preparing to withdraw his men, an arrow fired from inside the church struck down one of his men. Rage flew through the Campbell ranks and the church was set ablaze. With its thatched roof, the church burned quickly. Figures for the dead vary wildly, ranging from 20 to 160. Even by the standards of the day, the **Slaughter at Monzievaird** was considered a heinous crime. Several of the perpetrators were eventually brought to justice and beheaded at Stirling.

Around 1582, Dougal of Moidart entered Glen Lyon with a party of men set on stealing cattle to add to the herd already rustled by them from the Tryst at Falkirk. In the raid, two farmers, Campbells of Meggernie, were killed. In response, Duncan Campbell of Meggernie Castle and a strong force of clansmen followed the cattle trail to Glen Dochart where they ambushed the cattle thieves - **Ambush at Glen Dochart** (c.1582). The rustlers were captured, clad in irons and locked up at Meggernie. However, when Duncan Campbell brought the case to court, he failed to get a guilty verdict. Taking matters into his own hands, Campbell arranged for Douglas of Moidart to be shot and the other 36 prisoners to be hanged.

The MacGregors of Glenstrae, a notorious highland clan, were considered as so dangerous a group that the then king, James I (VI of Scotland), moved to counter their power and ability to operate. He firstly removed the clan's right to elect its own leader and subsequently proscribed the clan. The long list of the clan's offences is crowned by an event known as the Slaughter of Glen Fruin (7 February 1603). Over a period of two years, the MacGregors had successfully rustled cows, sheep and horses from the Colquhouns of Luss. On 7 February 1603, the MacGregors organised their biggest raid, stealing hundreds of animals and leaving many Colquhouns slaughtered in their wake. This forced the king to act and troops were dispatched against the clan. In

1610, a determined effort to tackle the MacGregors of Glenstrae was led by the Earl of Argyll. Over a three-year period, MacGregor's men were hunted down and killed and their women captured and branded. Those that survived the campaign against them did so by changing their names; many joined Clan Campbell.

Halfway along Loch Earn's southern bank and near to Ardvorlich House, lies a long stone upon which is inscribed:

> *Near this spot we re-interred the bodies of 7 McDonalds of Glencoe*
> *killed when attempting to harry Ardvorlich Anno Domino 1620.*

The McDonalds buried under the stone were part of a rustling party that had attempted to steal cattle belonging to the Stewarts of Ardvorlich House. In their **Raid of Ardvorlich** (1620), the McDonalds were defeated and seven of their clan perished. Initially, the bodies were thrown into a hole in the ground, but rediscovered many years later, their remains were reburied and the site marked.

NEAR ARDVORLICH HOUSE.

CHAPTER 6

WORLD WAR

A T THE VERY BEGINNING OF THE *First World War* (1914-1918), camps were constructed across Britain to imprison foreign nationals. These soon evolved into traditional prisoner-of-war (POW) camps. In Perthshire, POW camps were built at Balgowan, Drumbuach Wood (by Methven), Forgandenny, Glendevon and Strathardle (by Luncarty). Perth Prison was also utilised to house Axis prisoners. Agricultural work camps operated in several locations: Auchterarder, Forteviot, Keiloor, Kintillo, Leystone Farm and Tarrylow (by Balbeggie).

There were several *Second World War* (1939-45) POW camps built in Perthshire and these are listed below:

Balhary East near Alyth: Italian prisoners.
Calvine (Pitagowan) near Blair Atholl: Italian and (later)
    German prisoners; post-war a centre for displaced persons.
Cowden near Comrie: supply camp.
Cultybraggan near Comrie: maximum-security camp.
East Deanston near Doune: work camp.
Errol Airfield Camp (Pitroddie) near Errol: Italian, German and
    Austrian prisoners.
Findo Gask near Dunning: RAF camp.

Cultybraggan maximum-security POW camp was built and opened in 1939. It comprised five main compounds and a separate officer compound. Around 4000 category-A Italian and German prisoners-of-war were imprisoned at Cultybraggan during the camp's eight-year operation. Italian soldiers captured during the Western Desert campaigns were the first to be brought to Cultybraggan, but were subsequently relocated to allow higher security prisoners to be housed instead. These included members of the Afrika Corps and the SS, many of whom were ardent Nazis. For a period of the camp's operation, Polish soldiers guarded the camp under a very strict regime, which nevertheless was not as harsh as the manner in which senior German officers ruled their own men. In one infamous incident, a German POW, Sergeant Wolfgang Rosterg, accused of spying for the British, was condemned to death by his commanding officers and lynched. The case became a major media spectacle and eight of those involved with the killing were tried for murder; two were acquitted, one received a life sentence and the remaining five were hanged at Pentonville Prison. In 1944, a plot to free some of Cultybraggan's POWs was foiled and several German agents were themselves incarcerated at Cultybraggan. There is a suggestion that Rudolph Hess was imprisoned at Cultybraggan after his famous crash-landing in Scotland. There is no evidence to support this theory; he most likely spent his two nights in Scotland incarcerated at Buchanan Castle (by Kippen). Cultybraggan shut up shop as a POW camp in 1947. The camp was then utilised by the British Army (from 1949) as a training facility. A number of the camp's Second World War inmates were so taken by Scotland and its people that they elected to remain in the country after their release. At the end of the nineteen-eighties, Cultybraggan was nominated as the Regional Governmental HQ for Scotland in the event of a national emergency (such as nuclear war) and a nuclear bunker was constructed on the site. With the end of the Cold War, the camp was no longer needed and today is under the ownership of the Comrie Development Trust.

Not far from the site of the Battle of Sheriffmuir situated on the nearby moorland of Whitestone Rifle Range, close to the road, lie the remains of a section of a mock-up of the German Atlantic Wall defences. This extensive structure was designed to allow allied troops to be trained for the eventual D-Day Normandy Landings of June 1944. The wall, built in 1943, was an accurate copy of part of the actual German defences - based on aerial reconnaissance photographs. The dimensions of the Sheriffmuir Atlantic Wall were 86m (length) by 3m (height) and of varying width (0.5m-3m). The ground from the road to the wall was considered similar to the gently sloping beaches of Normandy; the road itself operated as a pretend coastline. East of the road, extensive defensive systems and structures were built and offensive structures were constructed to the west. The eastern defences include a reinforced concrete wall, an anti-tank ditch, bunkers and gun emplacements as well as hundreds of metres of trenches. A tramway operated across much of this side of the

SECOND WORLD WAR TANK.

complex. The offensive structures included gun emplacements and gun platforms linked by access tracks. Amongst the many military units that trained at Sheriffmuir were the 49th (West Riding) Infantry Division and the 52nd (Lowland) Division. The 1/4th Battalion King's Own Yorkshire Light Infantry were stationed in Crieff during their training at Sheriffmuir.

A smaller mock-up of the German North Atlantic coastal defences was built near Muthill. The 294 Field Company, Royal Engineers, constructed it.

Sheriffmuir's connection with military training extends back to the First World War when the 52nd (Lowland) Division utilised Whitestone Rifle Range in training for the Gallipoli landings. An extensive trench system was constructed across the moorland, these trenches acting as Turkish defensive lines.

The only known Second World War (1939-1945) bombing raid on Perth took place on the night of 26 June 1940. At 12.35am, a German bomb landed on Moncreiffe Tunnel. This was followed by six other bombs near to the Perth-Stanley Road. No one was hurt in the incidents. Perth Museum and Art Gallery is in possession of some of the bomb fragments from that raid:

1977.6.1 Vane of an incendiary bomb collected from the crater near the centre airshaft of Moncreiffe Tunnel. Size 120 x 50 mm
1977.6.2 Fragment of shrapnel collected as above. Size 200 x 80 x 15 mm

Elsewhere in Perthshire, German bombs landed in several locations: Fonab Moor, Dalreoch, Enochdhu, Balnacree Wood and Edradour.

A considerable body of Polish soldiers and pilots was stationed in Perthshire after the German Army's invasion of Poland and the fall of France in 1940. In all 20000 Polish troops were brought to the UK during the Second World War. Many remained within Perthshire until the end of the war whilst others were transported to the Soviet Union in 1941 to join the re-forming Polish Army. The Robert Douglas Memorial School in Scone was appropriated by the Poles as their HQ during their time in Perthshire. The Polish Eagle still graces that building today, now returned to use as a school. Other signage recognising the Poles' stay in this part of Scotland include substantial Polish War Graves in Wellshill Cemetery in Perth and a plaque outside the Perth and Kinross Registrar's Office at the foot of Tay Street, close to the River Tay. The Polish War Memorial in Welshill Cemetery bears the following inscription:

Eternal Glory to the Polish Soldiers Who Died in 1939-1945
For Our Freedom And Yours.

CHAPTER 7

A PERTHSHIRE
MILITARY MISCELLANY

A FEW EVENTS OF A MILITARY NATURE that have taken place in Perthshire do not fit easily into any of the previous chapters of this book. It is for this reason that this final chapter, *A Perthshire Military Miscellany*, exists to house them.

Skirmish on the North Inch (1443) - A minor skirmish took place on Perth's North Inch when John Gormac of Atholl, a captain of a gang of freebooters, attempted to rescue a prisoner being brought to Perth to be hanged. The prisoner who had earlier been found guilty of theft was in the charge of Sir William Ruthven, the Sheriff of Perth, and his officers. Both John Gormac and Sir William Ruthven were killed in the fight. Thirteen of Gormac's men also perished.

Raid into Atholl (late 1461) - Edward IV of England having made a pact with the Lord of the Isles set his new ally the task of subduing his unruly Scottish subjects. From his base at Castle Aros, on the Sound of Mull, the Lord of the Isles (self-proclaimed King of the Hebrides) raised a large force of soldiers under the command of his son, Angus, and Donald Balloch, which crossed to the mainland and marched on Inverness. After taking the castle, this marauding army rampaged across Atholl, attacked Blair Castle and seized the Earl and Countess of Atholl. In the raid, the chapel of St. Bridget (St. Bride) was violated, which subsequently caused Angus great feelings of guilt, compounded by the loss of many of his galleys in a storm between Lochaber and the islands. In an attempt to make amends for his religious crime and believing that he had earned the wrath of God, Angus released his prisoners, returned that which he had looted and underwent bare-foot penance in the desecrated chapel.

Burning of Weem Castle (1502) - Because of a dispute over the lands of Rannoch, Weem Castle was attacked and burned by Neil Stewart of Fortingall in 1502.

Battle of the Brig of Tay (22 July 1544) - Upon the Bridge of Perth, two groups of armed men, rival factions for the position of Perth Provost, came to blows. One side was supporters of John Charteris and Lord Gray of Kinfauns, the other, those around William Lord Ruthven. Dozens of men were killed before Ruthven's men carried the day. Lord Ruthven subsequently attained the position of Provost of Perth. The poet and historian Henry Adamson immortalised the Battle of the Brig of Tay in a verse written in 1638:

> *Within these bars were killed above three score,*
> *Upon the bridge and waters many more,*
> *But most of all did perish in the chase,*
> *For they pursued were onto the place*
> *Where all their baggage and their cannon lay,*
> *Which to the town was brought as lawful prey.*

Reformation and Counter-Reformation Events in Perthshire (May/June 1559) - John Knox, the Protestant reformer, entered Perth on 10 May 1559. On the 11th of that month he preached at St. John's Kirk a fiery sermon that so inflamed his receptive audience they formed a mob and proceeded to attack the religious houses of the town. The Carthusian monastery, the house of the Franciscan friars and that of the Dominican order, were all attacked and looted over a period of two days. Even St. John's Kirk did not escape their wrath. Church decorations, altars and ornaments were all destroyed by the rampaging mob. Perth, now a centre of dissident religious opinion, experienced an influx of supporters of John Knox. Mary Queen of Scots and her mother, the Queen Regent, Mary of Guise, were nearby watching the events. Their army, under the command of the Duke of Hamilton and Monsieur d'Oysel, stood at Auchterarder. Eventually, the decision was made to march on Perth and the town was occupied on 29 May 1559. When Knox spoke again in St. John's Kirk many members of the congregation were soldiers of the queen. This was a very tense period, but an agreement between the two sides was made. In return for the Queen Regent's promise neither to garrison Perth with French troops nor to persecute its residents, the followers of Knox agreed to leave. John Knox remained in Perth protected by dissident elements of the nobility. When it became clear that the French were paying the Scottish soldiers occupying Perth, Protestants from all over central Scotland poured back into the town. Feeling threatened and suffering desertions amongst her supporters, the Regent moved her army south to Dunbar.

Raid of Ruthven (23 August 1582) - It was while hunting in Atholl during the summer of 1582 that William Ruthven, 1st Earl of Gowrie, abducted the young James I (VI of Scotland). The royal prisoner was taken to and held at the Earl's residence, the House of Ruthven (Huntingtower Castle). Within a day of his seizure, James I (VI of Scotland) issued a proclamation declaring himself free to act and distancing himself from Catholicism and the Catholic Church's key figure close to the Crown, the Duke of Lennox. Ruthven's next move was to force the king into making him the head of a new ultra-Protestant government. This state of affairs lasted until June of 1583 when James I (VI of Scotland) succeeded in escaping his captors. Before another year was out William Ruthven was arrested and beheaded.

Perth Custom Rebellion (June 1592) - Local anger over the establishment of a new tax (imposed by Sir Robert Bruce) on goods in transit through Perth spilled over into violence. The dispute eventually came before the Perth Privy Council who ruled that both sides were equally at fault in the matter.

Incident at Carpow (28 September 1607) - Disputes between Perthshire's residents and the local council have been a common enough occurrence for centuries. Today the usual weapon of choice in any dispute is the pen or computer. This was not the case at Carpow in 1607, when a disagreement between the villagers and the council led to the local residents arming themselves and fighting a pitched battle against a force working for the local Baillies. There were extensive casualties on both sides including several deaths.

Riot at Muthill Kirk (3 August 1704) - William Hay was ordained Minister of Muthill on 3 August 1704. His ordination was not popular amongst many of the citizens of the village. These disgruntled members of the congregation armed with sword and stave proceeded to riot at the church. They took control of Muthill Kirk and its kirkyard and maintained control of both until the following summer (20 August 1705) at which time Minister Hay finally gained access to the church and its grounds.

Meal Mob Protests (1772-3) - Perthshire's harvest of 1772 was very poor, so that by the end of that year many locals were experiencing the effects of malnutrition. Despite the needs of the local populace, farmers and grain merchants still chose to export their products out of the county where they could make higher profits. In mid-December, when oatmeal supplies had dried up, armed resistance followed. Newburgh, just outside Perth, was the first scene of protest. On 21 December 400 armed villagers marched to the premises of a local corn factor, John Donaldson of Elcho. When the crowd spotted Donaldson, attempts were made to seize him, but he escaped. The hungry protestors next turned their attention to the grain exports. An attempt at preventing a grain ship from leaving Errol was made on Christmas Day. It was unsuccessful and the sixty-strong mob was forced to retreat. They returned with reinforcements but again failed to take the ship. Greater success was achieved on 30 December with the capture of a ship moored on Perth's New Shore. As the ship's cargo was being unloaded, members of the local militia under orders from the magistrates arrived. The crowd soon scattered. That night the rebellion escalated: John Scott's bakery in the town was ransacked at 3am and another Newburgh grain ship was seized. Two men captured by the authorities during the baker shop raid were placed in the prison at the end of the High Street. No sooner had word got out of the arrest, when a large force of rebels marched on the prison. Barring their way was a detachment of infantry, bayonets fixed, supported by cannon filled with grape shot. In front of the fully-armed soldiers, the rebels, armed only with sticks, stones and makeshift weaponry, did not waiver. Had the local magistrates' pragmatism not prevailed and the two prisoners not been released, many would have died on both sides. From the High Street, the victorious rebels, 400 strong, made their way to a corn granary at Elcho on the outskirts of Perth. Here they found the granary defended by 10 soldiers. Seeing the size of the force marching on the granary, the soldiers took their leave and retreated. Over 200 bolls of wheat were discovered, stockpiled by their greedy owner. Within a short time, local magistrates arrived at the grain store and pleaded with the rebels not to take the grain. Instead, a compromise was made by which the grain would be brought to the town the next day to be sold in the market. This action by the authorities only placated the hungry rebels for a few days. On Monday 4 January, a solo piper led a procession of demonstrators down Perth's High Street, across the River Tay and on to Balthayock. Aware that other farmers were still hiding their corn, the demonstrators broke into smaller units and marched on several farms: Glencarse, Mount Blair, Abernethy and Newburgh. In the following days, these expeditions of protest were copied in Dundee and Fife. In response, the authorities, under pressure from wealthy farmers and landowners to act, called in the army. Eighty dragoons from Linlithgow soon garrisoned the town. In the aftermath of the protests, the local authorities sought and attained revenge against those involved in direct action. Many found themselves arrested and brought to trial.

The following men, all from Perth, were tried at the High Court in Edinburgh on 15 March 1773:

Malcolm Cameron - guilty of pillage and rioting;

Peter Tosh - not guilty of pillage and rioting;

Thomas Wilkie - not guilty of pillage and rioting (non-appearance in court);

William Grant - not guilty of pillage and rioting (non-appearance in court)

James Bell - not guilty of pillage and rioting (non-appearance in court).

Sixteen men and two women were brought up to the Circuit Court in Perth on 28 April 1773. Two men and two women were found guilty and banished for life; the others were acquitted.

MUSKET BALLS FOUND CLOSE TO THE OLD BRIDGE ACROSS THE RIVER EARN.

Friends of the People and the United Scotsmen Risings and Rebellions (1792-97) - As the 18th century ended, political reform societies inspired by the French and American Revolutions and Thomas Paine's *The Rights of Man*, were set up throughout Britain. Of these societies, the Friends of the People was the most important and radical. By the end of 1792, almost 90 branches of the Friends were operating in Britain. Although independent of each other, the branches united periodically in conventions. In Perth, the inaugural meeting of the Friends of the People was held at the Guildhall (High Street, Perth) on 14 August 1792. Membership of the Perth branch was open to all, but in the main, hatters, weavers, tradesmen and a few clergymen filled its ranks. Just two months after its founding, the Perth branch could boast of 1200 members. Government persecution of the Friends of the People began in 1792 and continued for some time: its leaders were arrested, tried and in the case of Thomas Muir, a radical and popular Glasgow lawyer-turned-reformer, and others, transported to Australia. In response, the societies grew more radical and involved themselves in direct action and demonstrations. Perth was one of the centres for action. Large open-air meetings were held on the inches and support for the French Revolution reached fever pitch. When General Dumourier entered Brussels, a huge demonstration was arranged in Perth. A *'Tree of Liberty'* was raised in the town as demonstrators called for equality, liberty and the end of the monarchy. During the demonstration, the Duke of Atholl was spotted and forced by the hostile demonstrators to join them in their cries of *'Liberty and Fraternity'.*

For the entire night and the next day, the commandeered steeple bells of Perth rang in support of reform. Within the Perth Friends of the People, a militant tendency began to emerge. Secret correspondence with the National Assembly in France travelled from Perth to Paris. Arms were bought and stockpiled in Perth by the radicals. Revolution was in the air. Spies amongst the Friends' branches kept the police and government agents informed of developments and allowed individual leaders to be targeted. Despite the repression, the Perthshire radicals began to operate more openly. Henry Dundas, one of the most despised politicians of the day, was hanged in effigy at Scone, whilst in Perth a similar effigy was blown up with gunpowder. On 6 November 1792, demonstrators demanding the Duke of Atholl be sent to the guillotine picketed the Perth Hunt Ball. War with France brought economic recession to Britain and increased state repression that made the work of reforming groups extremely difficult. This drove the Friends of the People underground into small activist cells. Several cells operated in Perth, but despite their clandestine efforts, many Perth radicals found themselves victims of police informers and arrested. Perthshire at that moment was a volcano of revolutionary anger ready to blow. Armed men drilled in Auchterarder, a plan to stockpile 4000 pikes (the Pike Plot) led to arrests and trials for treason and links were made with the United Irishmen and to other European powers. A plan for 50000 Dutch troops to invade central Scotland on behalf of the radicals failed when the British Navy beat the Dutch fleet at the Battle of Camperdown in 1797. In the same year, the United Scotsmen proclaimed the start of the Scottish revolution, only to be crushed. The aftermath of this failure was brutal: reformist and revolutionary groups were proscribed and their leaders tried before the courts.

Anti-Militia Act Protests (1797) - The passing of the Militia (Conscription) Ballot Act of 1797 led to protests across Scotland. Under the act, men between the ages of 18 and 23 were liable to be conscripted by ballot. This was a very unpopular law and the administrators of the conscription became the targets of activists. Local schoolmasters were charged by the State with drawing up suitable conscription lists and consequently many found themselves threatened with violence and reprisals. At Fincastle, activists attacked the local schoolmaster (Forbes) cutting off one of his ears with a scythe. Elsewhere, at Moulin, another schoolmaster, a Mr Robertson, had his parish register stolen by protestors. Anti-Militia Act protestors in Perthshire did not merely satisfy themselves with dealing with minor officials: even the Deputy Lieutenant of the county was warned to cease organising conscription locally. The most significant anti-Militia Act event involved local members of the

United Scotsmen. A small rebel army raised amongst the United Scotsmen's supporters in Perthshire marched on Castle Menzies under their commander Cameron, a wright from the parish of Weem, and his second-in-command, James Menzies Junior, a local merchant. The castle was easily surrounded and the Duke of Atholl captured. Under threat, the Duke agreed not to implement the Militia Act until he had consulted the populace of Perthshire. As government troops poured into the county the rebels were forced to abandon their activities.

Napoleonic Wars (1799-1815) - One consequence of the Napoleonic Wars was the problem of housing the thousands of prisoners that such a pan-European conflict generated. Camps were constructed across the British mainland as prisons for these POWs, who in the main were French. Sissinghurst Castle, Norman Cross, Liverpool, Portchester, Greenlaw-Valleyfield, Stapleton-Bristol, Forton-Porstmouth, Milbray-Plymouth, Dartmoor and Perth were all locations for these camps. In Perth, the POW camp was situated where Perth Prison stands today; it was known as the Perth Depot and was built in 1812 with a capacity of 7000 prisoners. Ordinary soldiers were housed in five three-level buildings (130ft by 30ft), each with a capacity of 1140 men, arranged around a central square and surrounded by iron palisades. Within these units space was so tight that prisoners were forced to organise special sleeping arrangements. The French prisoners lay on their bunks making the shape of a spoon with turning done under command and by entire ranks at a time. Petty officers were placed in their own unit (capacity 1100). A separate hospital building was located on the site and could cater for up to 150 patients. Around the prison complex stood a 12 foot 6 inch high wall supported in its function by a further iron palisade. The area between the two walls was patrolled by sentries who formed part of the 300 strong guards that made up the three militia units based at Perth Depot. In the very centre of the prison, a market place was created so that prisoners could purchase produce brought in by local farmers and artisans. The skilful forging of banknotes and coins to buy produce from the market was very common. Four hundred prisoners, the depot's first residents, arrived in August of 1812. Their journey from Plymouth to Perth was firstly by sea to Dundee and then overland. Later, prisoners were dropped at Kirkcaldy and then marched to Perth. A small minority of the Perth Depot's inmates was made up of women. Escape attempts were very common, though few were successful. Only a month after the first arrivals, an escapee made it as far as a field in nearby Friarton. By 26 August 1813, Perth Depot was running at capacity. Eventually, with the first defeat of Napoleon and the capture of Paris in 1814, the prisoners were repatriated, travelling home from Newburgh by ship. The prison was closed on 31 July 1814. Between 1815 and 1833 the prison operated as a military clothing warehouse. After that period it evolved into a General Prison and maintains that function today.

Ambush at Corrymuckloch (21 December 1831) - Corrymuckloch is a small village north of Crieff and about two miles from Amulree. A few days before the Christmas of 1831, a party of smugglers handling barrels of untaxed whisky were caught in the act at Corrymuckloch by a squadron of Royal Scots Greys. Despite being surprised by the heavily-armed dragoons, the smugglers battled their way out of the ambush and got away.

Battle over Glen Tilt (13 August 1847) - Professor John Balfour, a well-known 19th century academic, whilst leading a geographical field trip to Glen Tilt, found his party's path physically blocked through the glen by a group of ghillies. The ghillies were under orders from the local laird to prevent the geographers from crossing his land. Although the confrontation ended without bloodshed, the battle continued in the courts. It eventually reached the House of Lords, where Professor Balfour was successful in gaining a positive judgement in favour of the concept of right of way. The significance of their ruling extended far beyond Glen Tilt; it set an important legal precedent.

Dunkeld Toll Rebellion (c.1858) - The Bridge at Dunkeld was constructed in 1809. For the next 70 years a toll was levied for its use. Increasingly over this period, the populace of Dunkeld and Birnam grew resentful of the toll. This discontent manifested itself in physical acts of rebellion on more than one occasion. When the Scottish Midland Junction Railway built a station on the other side of the River Tay from the town in 1856, toll discontent intensified. It reached its climax after the splits within the Protestant Church (the Disruption). The closest Free Church to Dunkeld was in Birnam. In order to worship in their church of choice, many Dunkeld residents were forced to pay the toll. A key figure in the campaign against the toll resided at Dundonnachie House and so the direct action taken by anti-toll protestors became known as the Dundonnachie Toll Riots. The most striking aspect of the rebellion was the blowing up of the Duke of Atholl's folly that over looked a small waterfall of the River Braan in the Hermitage (by Dunkeld), a natural-looking garden landscape created by the Dukes of Atholl in the 18th century.

BIBLIOGRAPHY

Abbott, Donald M. *Pitroddie Perspective.*
Perth: Friends of Perth and Kinross Council Archive, 2003.

Abell, Francis *Prisoners of war in Britain, 1756 to 1825.*
Oxford: Oxford University Press, 1914.

Aberdeen (Burgh) *Extracts from the Council Register of the Burgh of Aberdeen 1643-1747.*
Edinburgh: Scottish Burgh Records Society, 1872.

Aitchison, Nick *Forteviot A Pictish and Scottish Royal Centre.* Stroud: Tempus, 2006.

Alcock, L. *The north Britons, the Picts and the Scots* in Casey, J., *The end of Roman Britain, Archaeological Reports,* BAR British, volume 71, 1979.

A Memorial to the Battle of Tibbermuir. 1877. AK Bell Library, Perth.

Annals of Iona.

Annals of Ulster.

Anon. *Scottish Battles.* Newtongrange: Langsyne Publishers, 1985.

Archibald, Malcolm *Scottish Battles, Chambers mini guides.* Edinburgh: Chambers, 1990.

Argyll, Duke of, Scotland *As it was and as it is.* Edinburgh: David Douglas, 1887.

Armstrong, Pete *The battle of Dupplin Moor 1332.*
Hobilar - Journal of the Lance and Longbow Society, volume 45, 2000.

Barrow, Geoffrey W. S. *Robert Bruce and the community of the realm of Scotland.*
Edinburgh: Edinburgh University Press, 1988.

Barthorp, Michael and Embleton, G. A. *The Jacobite rebellions, 1689-1745.*
Oxford: Osprey Publications Limited, 1992.

Barty, Alexander *The history of Dunblane.* Stirling: Stirling District Libraries, 1994.

Baxter, Peter *Perth: past and present. Volume 1 and 2.* Perth: John McKinlay, 1928.

Beresford Ellis, Peter *Macbeth: High King of Scotland 1040-57.*
London: Frederick Muller Ltd., 1980.

Bingham, Caroline *The kings and queens of Scotland.*
London: Weidenfield and Nicolson, 1976.

Black, C. Stewart *Scottish battles.* Glasgow: Brown Son and Ferguson, 1936.

Brander, Michael and **Macgregor, Jimmie** *Scottish and Border battles and ballads.*
London: Seeley, 1975.

Broderick, Mike *The Marquis of Montrose and the Battle of Tippermuir.*
Paper presented to 1st Marquis of Montrose Society,
www.montrose-society.org.uk/batti.htm.

Brotchie, T. C. F. *The battlefields of Scotland: their legend and story.*
New York: Dodge Publishing, 1913.

Broun, Davit, Finlay, R. J. and **Lynch, Michael** *Image and Identity:
the making and re-making of Scotland throughout the ages.*
Edinburgh: John Donald Publishers Ltd., 1998.

Brown, Chris *The Battle for Aberdeen.* Stroud: Tempus, 2002.

Brown, Chris *William Wallace: The true story of Braveheart.* Stroud: Tempus, 2005.

Brown, Chris *Scottish Battlefields.* Stroud: Tempus, 2008.

Brown, P. Hume *History of Scotland, (volume II).*
Cambridge: Cambridge University Press, 1902.

Brown, Reverend Thomas *Notes relating to Dunsinnane Hill.* Edinburgh:
Proceedings of the Society of Antiquaries of Scotland, volume 9, 1870-72.

Buchan, John *The Marquis of Montrose.*
London: Thomas Nelson and Sons Limited, 1913.

Buchan, John *Oliver Cromwell.* London: Hodder and Stoughton, 1934.

Burrow, Ed. J. *Picturesque Perthshire.*
Cheltenham: Ed. J. Burrow & Company, Limited, 1932.

Burton, John, Hill *The history of Scotland, from Agricola's invasion to the extinction of
the last Jacobite insurrection.* Edinburgh: William Blackwood and Sons, 1898.

Burton, J. H. *History of Scotland.* Edinburgh: William Blackwood and Sons, 1905.

Caldwell, David H. *Scottish weapons and fortifications 1100-1800.*
Edinburgh: John Donald Publishers Limited, 1981.

Cameron, A. D. *Discover Scotland's history.* Edinburgh: Oliver & Boyd, 1963.

Cameron, Nancy Foy *The Clans of Atholl.* Blair Atholl: Atholl Brown, 1995.

Cameron, Nancy Foy *What really happened at Killiecrankie.*
Pitlochry: Atholl Browse Publications, 1998.

Campbell, Duncan *Book of Garth and Fortingall.* Inverness: Northern Counties, 1888.

Carlton, Charles *Charles I the personal monarch.*
London: Routledge & Kegan Paul, 1983.

Carment, S. *Scenes and Legends of Comrie and Upper Strathearn.*
Dundee: James P. Matthews, 1882.

Cary, Henry *Memorials of the Great Civil War in England from 1646 to 1652,
Volumes I and II.* London: Henry Colburn Publishers, 1842.

Chalmers, George *Caledonia (8 volumes).* Paisley: Alexander Gardner, 1894.

Chambers, Robert *A Biographical Dictionary of Eminent Scotsmen (3 volumes).*
London: Blackie and Son, 1875.

Cheape, Hugh *Tartan: the Highland habitat.*
Edinburgh: National Museums of Scotland, 1991.

Christison, D. *The forts, camps and other field-works of Perth, Forfar and Kincardine.*
Edinburgh: Proceedings of the Society of Antiquaries of Scotland, volume 34, 1910.

Chronology of Perth, 1114-1900. Perth: AK Bell Local Studies Library, 1995.

Clark, David *Battlefield walks: Scotland.* Stroud: Sutton Publishing, 1996.

Coutts, Herbert *Tayside before History.*
Dundee: Dundee Museum and Art Gallery, 1971.

Cowan, Edward, J. *Montrose. For covenant and king.*
London: Weidenfield and Nicolson, 1977.

Cowan, Samuel *Ancient Capital of Scotland, volume 1.*
London: Simpkin, Marshall, Hamilton, Kent & Company, 1904.

Cowan, W. *Rambles in Scotland.* Dumfries: Courier, 1933.

Cunningham, Audrey *The loyal clans.* Cambridge: Cambridge University Press, 1932.

Davie, J. W. *An Historical Atlas of Scotland c.400 - c.1600.* 1925.

Donaldson, Gordon *Common Errors in Scottish History.*
London: George Philip & Son Limited, 1956.

Donaldson, Gordon and **Morpeth, Robert S.** *A Dictionary of Scottish History.*
Edinburgh: John Donlad Publishers Limited, 1977.

Duncan, Jeremy *Perth and Kinross. The Big County.*
Edinburgh: John Donald Publishers Limited, 1997.

Duncan, Jeremy *Perth: A Century of Change - The Fair City 1900-2000.*
Derby: Breedon Books Publishing, 2008.

Dunkeld and Birnam. Dunkeld and Birnam Mercantile Association, 1923.

Evans, Martin Marix *The Military Heritage of Britain and Ireland.*
London: Andre Deutsch, 1998.

Fergusson, Charles *Sketches of the early history, legends and traditions of
Strathearn and its glens.* Gaelic Society of Inverness, c.1880.

Firth, Charles Harding (editor) *Memoirs of the Duke and Duchess of Newcastle.*
London: John C. Nimmo, 1886.

Fittis, Robert S. *Burgh Records.* Perth.

Fittis, Robert S. *Selections from the Scots Magazine.*

Fittis, Robert S. *The Mercer Family.* AK Bell Library, Perth.

Fittis, Robert S. *Antiquarian Miscellany.* Perth, 1875.

Fittis, Robert S. *Sheriff Court Records.* Perth, 1875.

Fittis, Robert S. *Historical and Traditionary Gleanings Concerning Perthshire.*
Perth, 1876.

Fittis, Robert S. *Chronicles of Perthshire.* Perth, 1877.

Fittis, Robert S. *Sketches of Olden Times in Perthshire.* Perth, 1878.

Fittis, Robert S. *Laws and Acts of the Chapmen of Perthshire.* 1879.
AK Bell Library, Perth.

Fittis, Robert S. *Chronicles of Perthshire.* Perth, 1890.

Forbes, George *Scottish battles: 86 AD to 1746.* Glasgow: Lang Syne, 1996.

Forth Naturalist and Historian. Stirling: Stirling University.

Fraser, Antonia *Mary Queen of Scots.* London: World Books, 1969.

Furgol, Edward, M. *A regimental history of the Covenanting Armies, 1639-1651.*
Edinburgh: John Donald Publishers Limited, 1990.

Gardiner, Samuel R. *History of the Great Civil War. (3 volumes).*
London: Longmans, Green and Company, 1886-1891.

Gibb, Mildred Ann *The Lord General. A life of Thomas Fairfax.*
London: Lindsay Drummond, 1938.

Gordon, John (editor), *The New Statistical Account of Scotland Volume X Perth (Parish of Tibbermore by Rev. Weir Tulloch).* Edinburgh: William Blackwood and Sons, 1845.

Gordon of Ruthven, Patrick *A short abridgement of Britane's distemper.*
Aberdeen: Spalding Club, 1844.

Graham-Campbell, David *Perth. The Fair City.*
Edinburgh: John Donald Publishers Limited, 1994.

Graham-Campbell, David *Scotland's Story in her Monuments.*
London: Robert Hale, 1982.

Grant, J. *British Battles on Land and Sea (3 volumes).*
Cassel, Peter, Galpin and Company, 1895.

Green, Howard *The battlefields of Britain and Ireland.* London: Constable, 1973.

Gregg, Pauline *King Charles I.* London: Dent, 1981.

Guest, Ken and **Guest, Denise** *British Battles.* London: Collins, 1996.

Hamilton, J. *Scottish Battles.* New Lanark: Geddes and Grosset, 2004.

Hay, M. D. *Reminiscences of Tibbermore and District.* Cultmalundie, 1927.

Higham, F. M. G. *Charles I.* London: Hamish Hamilton, 1932.

Hill, Christopher *The English Revolution 1640.*
London: Lawrence and Wishart Limited, 1940.

Hill, James Michael *Celtic Warfare 1595-1760.*
Edinburgh: John Donald Publishers Limited, 1986.

Hogg, James *Tales of the Wars of Montrose.* Edinburgh: Edinburgh University Press, 1996.

Honeyman, Valerie *Perth: A Very Dangerous Place?: Radicalism in Perth in the 1790s.*
Perth and Kinross Council Archives, 2003.

Hunter, Thomas *Illustrated Guide to Perthshire.*
Perth: Henderson, Robertson and Hunter, 1886.

Hunter, Thomas *Illustrated Guide to Perthshire.*
Perth: Henderson, Robertson and Hunter, 1897.

Index to the Records Belonging to the Magistrates and Council of the Burgh of Perth of Acts and Other Proceedings as Relative to the Burgh Drawn up in the Year 1831.
AK Bell Library, Perth.

Inglis, Bill *The Battle of Sheriffmuir.* Stirling: Stirling Council Libraries, 2005.

In Scotland (magazine), *Historic Dunning.* 2005.

Insh, George P. *The Study of Local History and other Essays.*
Edinburgh: Educational Institute of Scotland, 1932.

Jackson, Anthony *The Pictish Trail.* Orkney: Orkney Press Limited, 1989.

Keay, John and **Keay, Julia** (editors), *Collins Encyclopaedia of Scotland.*
London: Harper Collins, 1991.

Kenyon, John and **Ohlmeyer, Jane** (editors), *The civil wars. A military history of England, Scotland and Ireland 1638-1660.* Oxford: Oxford University Press, 1998.

Kinross, John *Discovering Scottish battlefields.* Aylesbury: Shire Press, 1986.

Kinross, John *Discovering Scottish battlefields of England and Scotland.*
Buckinghamshire: Shire Press, 1998.

Knight, Gary *The Battle of Methven.* Perth: For the Lion, 2006.

Lang, Andrew *A History of Scotland from the Roman Occupation (4 volumes).*
Edinburgh and London: William Black and Sons, 1907.

Lang, Andrew *A Short History of Scotland.*
Edinburgh: William Blackwood and Sons, 1911.

Liddell, Colin *Pitlochry. A History.* Aberfeldy: Watermill, 2008.

Linklater, Eric *The Survival of Scotland.* London: Heinemann, 1968.

Love, Dane *Scottish kirkyards.* London: Robert Hale, 1989.

Mackenzie, Agnes Mure *The Passing of the Stewarts.*
Edinburgh: Oliver and Boyd Limited, 1937.

Mackintosh of Mackintosh, Margaret *The clan Mackintosh and the clan Chattan.*
Edinburgh: W & A. K. Johnston, 1948.

MacLaren, Moray *Bonnie Prince Charlie.* Herts: Granada Publishing Limited, 1974.

Malcolm, David *A genealogical memoir of the most noble and ancient House of Drummond.*
Edinburgh: G. Maxwell, 1808.

Marchioness of Tullibardine (editor), *Military History of Perthshire 1660-1902.*
Perth: R. A. & J. Hay, 1908.

Marchioness of Tullibardine (editor), *Military History of Perthshire.* 1899-1902.
Perth: R. A. & J. Hay, 1908.

Matthews, Rupert *England versus Scotland, The great British battles.*
Barnsley: Leo Cooper, 2003.

Marshall, William *Historic Scenes in Perthshire.*
Edinburgh: Oliphant, Anderson and Fernier, 1881.

McKerracher, Archie *Perthshire in History and Legend.*
Edinburgh: John Donald Publishers Limited, 2000.

McMichael, George *Notes on the Way Through the Counties of Perth, Clackmannan, Forfar and Kincardine.* Ayr: Hugh Henry.

McNeill, Peter G. B. and **MacQueen, Hector L.** *Atlas of Scottish History to 1707.*
Edinburgh: The Scottish Medievalists & Department of Geography,
University of Edinburgh, 1996.

McNeill, Peter and **Nicholson, Ranald** *An historical atlas of Scotland, c.400-c.1600.*
St. Andrews: Committee of the Conference of Scottish Medievalists, 1975.

Meldrum, Neil *Forteviot. The History of Strathearn Parish.*
Paisley: Alexander Gardner, 1926.

Mitchell, John Fowler and **Mitchell, Sheila Scott** *Monumental Inscriptions
(pre-1855) in South Perthshire.* Scottish Genealogy Society, 1974.

Iain, Moncreiffe *The Highland Clans - The dynastic origins, chiefs and background of
the Clans and of some other families connected with Highland history.*
London: Barrie and Jenkins, 1977.

Moody, David *Scottish Local History.* London: B. T. Batsford, 1986.

Murray, John, Seventh Duke of Atholl *Chronicles of the Atholl and Tullibardine
(volume 1).* Edinburgh: Privately Printed, 1908.

Murray, Katharine Marjory *A Military History of Perthshire 1660-1902.*
Perth: R. A. & J. Hay, 1908.

Ordnance Survey Map of Roman Britain. 3rd Edition. O.S., 1956.

Ordnance Survey Map of Britain in the Dark Ages. 2nd Edition. O.S., 1971.

Omand, Donald *The Perthshire Book.* Edinburgh: Birlinn, 1999.

Ormonde Manuscripts, *Nominal Roll of the Officers that left Ireland with
Alasdair MacColla. Sent by Lord Antrim to Lord Ormonde 15 November 1644.*
National Library, Dublin.

Our Heritage Car Trails. From Blairgowrie to Pitlochry and Dunkeld.
Blairgowrie: Blairgowrie and Rattray Community Council, 1996.

Ouston, Hugh (editor), *A History of the Scottish People, 1450-1840.*
GB: Learning and Teaching Scotland, 2000.

Paton, Donald N. M. *Twixt Castle and Mart. The Story of Needless Road.*
Perth: Perth and Kinross Libraries, 2005.

Paton, Henry *The Clan Campbell.* Edinburgh: Otto Schulze and Company, 1914.

Peacock, David *Perth: Its annals and its archives.* Perth: Thomas Richardson, 1849.

Peacock, Edward (editor), *Army Lists of the Roundheads and Cavaliers.*
London: Chatto & Windus, 1874.

Pearson, John MacMillan *Around Perth.* Perth: John MacMillan Pearson, 2003.

Perth and Kinross Libraries, *Alert! The War Years in Perth.*
Perth: Perth and Kinross Libraries, 1989.

Perth Advertiser

Perth Burgh Records 1421-1902 (B59). AK Bell Library, Perth.

Perth Courier

Perthshire - the official county guide. Perth: County Council of Perth, 1953.

Petegorsky, David W. *Left-wing democracy in the English Civil War.*
Stroud: Alan Sutton, 1995.

Petrie, Charles (editor), *The Letters, Speeches and Proclamations of King Charles I.*
London: Cassell & Company, 1935.

Prebble, John *Glencoe. The Story of the Massacre.* London: Secker and Warburg, 1966.

Peterson, Edward *The Message of Scotland's Symbol Stones.*
Perthshire: PCD Ruthven Books, 1996.

Reid, A. G. *Annals of Auchterarder and memorials of Strathearn.*
Perth: Perth and Kinross District Libraries, 1989.

Reid, Stuart *Killiecrankie 1689.* Leigh-on-Sea: Partizan Press, 1989.

Reid, Stuart *The Campaigns of Montrose.* Edinburgh: The Mercat Press, 1990.

Reid, Stuart *Scots armies of the English civil wars.* Oxford: Osprey Publishing, 1999.

Reid, Stuart *Auldearn 1645: the Marquis of Montrose's Scottish campaign.*
Oxford: Osprey Publishing, 2003.

Rogers, Charles *Monuments and monumental inscriptions in Scotland (volume 2).*
London: Charles Griffin & Company, 1872.

Roots, Ivan *The Great Rebellion, 1642-60.* London: B. T. Batsford, 1966.

Rose, Iain *The Jacobites.* Hove: Wayland Publishers, 1995.

Royle, Trevor *Discover Scotland* (magazine), volume 4, part 43.
The Battle of Sheriffmuir.

Sadler, John *Scottish Battles: From Mons Graupius to Culloden.*
Edinburgh: Canongate, 1996.

Terry, Charles Sanford (editor), *Papers relating to the Army of the Solemn league
and covenant 1643-1647.* Edinburgh: Scottish History Society, 1917.

Scottish Historical Review, volume 1, 1903, *Monzievaird conflict of 1490.*
Glasgow: James Maclehose and Sons.

Scottish Historical Review, volume 49, 1970, *The movements of Robert the Bruce
between September 1307 and May 1308.* Aberdeen: Aberdeen University Press.

Seymour, W. B. *Battles in Britain (two volumes).* Sidgwick and Jackson, 1975.

Shearer, John E. *The battlefields around Stirling.* Stirling: R. S. Shearer and Son, 1913.

Sinclair, Sir John *The Statistical Account of Scotland 1791-1799 (volume XI)*. Wakefield: EP Publishing Limited, 1976.

Small, Alan and **Thomas, Lisbeth M.** *The Picts in Tayside. 1987.*

Smith, D. Crawford *The Historians of Perth*. Perth: John Christie, 1906.

Smith, Gavin and **Smith, Ruth** *Scotland in Old Photographs*. Stroud: Sutton Publishers Limited, 2000.

Smurthwaite, David *The Complete Guide to the Battlefields of Britain*. London: Mermaid, 1993.

Stavart, Marion L. *Perth. A Short History*. Perth: Perth and Kinross District Libraries, 1991.

Stevenson, David (editor), *The Government of Scotland Under the Covenanters 1637-1651*. Edinburgh: Scottish Historical Society, 1982.

Stevenson, David *Highland Warrior: Alasdair MacColla and the civil wars*. Edinburgh: Saltire Society, 1994.

Stevenson, David *King or Covenant? Living in Troubled Times*. Edinburgh: Tuckwell Press Limited, 1996.

Stevenson, J. H. (editor), *The Scottish Antiquary* (volume XIV). Edinburgh: George P. Johnson, 1900.

Stewart, Elizabeth *Dunkeld. Ancient City*. Coupar Angus: William Culross and Son Limited, 1979.

SUAT, *Perth. The archaeology of the medieval town*. Perth: SUAT, 1984.

Tabraham, Christopher *Scotland BC*. Edinburgh: HMSO, 1988.

Taylor, David B. (editor), *Third Statistical Account of Scotland (volume 27)*. Coupar Angus: Culross the Printers, 1979.

The Statistical Account of Perthshire. Edinburgh: William Blackwood and Sons, 1894.

Tomasson, Katherine and **Buist, Francis** *Battles of the '45*. London: B. T. Batsford Limited, 1962.

Transactions and Proceedings of the Perthshire Society of Natural Science. Perth, 1881-1954.

Warner, Philip *Famous Scottish Battles*. London: Cooper, 1995.

Wedgwood, C. V. *Montrose*. London: Collins, 1952.

Wedgwood, C. V. *The King's War 1641-1647*. London: Collins, 1958.

Wheeler, Hilary *Aberfeldy to Glenlyon*. Aberfeldy: Appin, 1981.

Wheeler, Hilary *Killin to Glencoe*. Aberfeldy: Appin, 1982.

Wheeler, James Scott *The Irish and British wars 1637-1654*. London: Routledge, 2002.

Willcock, John *The Great Marquess. Life and times of Archibald, 8th Earl, and 1st (and only) Marquess of Argyll (1607-1661)*. Edinburgh: Oliphant & Company, 1903.

Williams, Ronald *Montrose. cavalier in mourning.* London: B & Jenkins, 1975.

Wilson, George *The Annals of the Glover Incorporation 1300-1905.*
Perth: R. A. and Hay, J., 1905.

Wilson, John *Dunning. Its Parochial History.* Crieff: D. Philips, 1906.

Wishart, George *Memoirs of James, Marquis of Montrose. 1639-1650.*
London: Longman Green 1893.

Young, Brigadier P. and **Adair, J.** *Hastings to Culloden.*
London: G. Bell and Sons, 1964.

Young, John R. *Celtic dimensions of the British civil war.*
Edinburgh: John Donald Publishers Limited, c.1997.

Killiecrankie Visitor Centre

Museum of Abernethy

Perth Museum and Art Gallery

www.alternative-perth.co.uk

www.battlefieldstrust.com

www.montrose-society.org.uk

www.pkht.org.uk

www.rcahms.gov.uk

INDEX OF NAMES & PLACES